THE PLAYER KING

By the same author
(with others)
An Introduction to Chaucer

As Editor
The Elizabethan Voyages

Three Elizabethan Plays

The General Prologue to The Canterbury Tales

The Descent of Euphues

Religio Medici

Andrew Marvell: Some Poems

THE
PLAYER KING

*A Theme of Shakespeare's
Histories*

by

JAMES WINNY

1968

CHATTO & WINDUS
LONDON

Published by
Chatto & Windus Ltd
40 William IV Street
London W.C.2
*
Clarke, Irwin & Co. Ltd
Toronto

SBN: 7011 1316 2

PR
2982
W5

56587

In memory of my Mother

Contents

Line-references of passages quoted from Shakespeare's works are taken from the New Arden edition. Passages taken from the editorial commentary of *Henry IV Part I* are identified by the name of the editor, Professor A. R. Humphreys.

CHAPTER I

Introduction

SHAKESPEARE's history plays seem to have been un-
fortunate at their literary christening. Alone among
the poet's works they were given a name which suggests
a primary interest not literary but political, and which
implies an intention of using drama in order to present an
interpretation of historical events. Whether or not
Heminge and Condell meant to be understood in this
sense, the implication has remained; suggesting that the
Histories are unlike the Tragedies and Comedies not
merely in matter but in kind. More recently they have
been found to embody Shakespeare's considered views
on government, order and degree; and the two tetralogies,
so called in deference to this reading, have been read as
Shakespeare's moral commentary on the consequences of
deposing a divinely appointed monarch. The interpretation has the possible attraction of placing Shakespeare
firmly on the side of the political establishment, as
unofficial spokesman for the authority of Tudor government. A reader content with this estimate of Shakespeare
is unlikely to object that such an approach exalts the
political and moral elements of work whose first characteristic is imaginative. The early plays, it could be argued,
contain little of poetic interest.

It might be critically profitable to make a fresh start
with the Histories, by recognising that the dramatic
category devised for them by Shakespeare's editors does
not represent such a difference of kind as exists between

9

tragedy and comedy. By classifying a play as a History they did no more than indicate its subject-matter very broadly, offering no opinion on the view of life which it presented. *Richard III* has as much claim to be considered a tragedy as a history-play, and *Henry IV* is better characterised as an ironic comedy. *Macbeth*, an undisputed tragedy, was drawn from the same chronicle source as supplied the dramatic stuff of many of the Histories, and was treated by Tillyard as a later play of this category. This was surely mistaken. The Histories are works of an indeterminate literary kind, capable of extension towards either the comic or the tragic. As such, they provided a medium in which Shakespeare's rapidly developing powers as poet could be exercised, by ranging over an unrestricted field of events. It seems significant that all these plays except *Henry VIII*, a work of late collaboration, belong to the early phase of Shakespeare's career. He abandoned the genre when he was about to prove his full creative power in plays whose material is more purposefully selected and organised.

It may still be necessary to insist that, like the rest of Shakespeare's work, the history plays are essentially imaginative in character. Interpretation based on the assumption that they are plays about political ambition, kingship, neglect of rule, and the kindred subjects which offer themselves as explicit issues of the Histories, usually yields an intelligible reading. But it leaves much unexplained, and does not satisfy the need to establish Shakespeare's total meaning, through a reading of the play which takes into account not a few prominent features but all the poetic and dramatic elements on which he has imposed a unified structure of relationships. By such analysis we may hope to reveal the imaginative design of the play, and to identify the centres of interest upon which its attention converges. It may not be easy to accept this as the meaning of the play, but much Shakespeare criticism is mistaken about the nature of the message which the poet's work can be expected to transmit. Shakespeare's imaginative activity consists of connecting and relating together, not of singling out. We begin to understand his plays only when we have traced out the design which integrates so many scattered images and events: elements which take their meaning from their poetic environment, and lose it when isolated. This book attempts to follow the imaginative design of the later history plays; *Richard II*, the two parts of *Henry IV*, and *Henry V*.

The tendency to look for an explicit moral purpose in the Histories may have been encouraged by their position in the canon, and by the habit of regarding the first six or seven years of Shakespeare's career as a period of creative immaturity. Some of the early plays have the crude energy of talent not yet harnessed to a disciplined purpose; but although the verse movement and the dramatic development of the early Histories are often stiff and uncouth, Shakespeare's imagination is already impressing characteristic forms upon his material. The tumultuousness that is so marked in *Henry VI* crowds the stage with a mass of events and with animated figures who in themselves embody an imaginative view of life. Within this dramatic hurly-burly the mature poet repeatedly hints at himself. Concepts may be awkwardly presented, and the action may develop cumbrously, as though Shakespeare had given only rough form to massive ideas; but the imaginative pressure behind manifests itself unmistakably. The plays lack finish, not energy and purpose. If there is a period of apprenticeship, it relates to Shakespeare's acquiring technical mastery of a complex medium. In his later writing his imaginative outlook takes on new depths and insights, but does not move far from the basic positions it had assumed in his earliest work. The first expression of these seminal ideas, which are carried forward into the greater plays that follow, gives the first Histories a special interest.

The characteristic imaginative outlook and concerns of the young Shakespeare are represented, almost in a literal sense of the term, in a passage of *The Rape of Lucrece*; an early work rich in what might now be called pre-echoes of Shakespeare's mature interests. The passage [lines 1366–1456] describes a picture in which Lucrece seeks and finds an image of her own grief and despair. This ambitious work, 'made for Priam's Troy', depicts various characters and incidents of the Trojan War, culminating in the fall of the city. Its comprehensive survey includes scenes depicting the Trojan army marching to battle, Nestor addressing the Greek soldiers, Sinon insinuating himself into Priam's trust, and Hecuba lamenting over the king's insulted body; with no regard to narrative chronology. Since Lucrece can examine only one scene at a time the incoherence of the whole picture is not apparent: instead, there is an effect of dramatic profusion and vitality. Shakespeare builds up the painting piecemeal, in terms appropriate to his own art where each successive scene provides changes of subject-matter and emotional colour; making his painter a dramatist. References to the artist's power of giving life to inanimate things initiate a sense of creative activity, which Lucrece supports by acting-out the experience which the painter describes, as partner in his work:

INTRODUCTION

So Lucrece set a-work sad tales doth tell
To pencill'd pensiveness and coloured sorrow;
She lends them words, and she their looks doth borrow.
                                        1496–8

Its confusion of subject-matter and chronology make this
'piece of skilful painting' an implausible masterpiece;
but in its heroic scale and dignity, its copiousness and
extravagant feeling, the work is immediately suggestive of
Shakespeare. Lucrece is scrutinising a pictorial equivalent
of one of the history plays.

The picture is crowded with action, made lurid by
physical violence and hectic emotion. Blood reeks and
dying eyes gleam; pioneers labour, begrimed with sweat;
Trojan mothers watch their sons leave the city, torn
between pride and anxiety; besieged men peer wanly
through loopholes at a daunting enemy, and a crowd
hanging on Nestor's words seethes angrily as men fight
for a view of the speaker. Nothing is still, and every
detail of the huge work suggests a state of vigorous
happening, as the artist imparts an impression of movement and sensation to all his figures. By using a kind of
graphic shorthand he is able to introduce many more
characters and incidents than could be fully described in a
restricted space; cramming his picture with fragmentary
forms that suggest complete figures:

> For much imaginary work was there;
> Conceit deceitful, so compact, so kind,
> That for Achilles' image stood his spear,
> Gripp'd in an armed hand; himself, behind,
> Was left unseen, save to the eye of mind:
>   A hand, a foot, a face, a leg, a head,
>   Stood for the whole to be imagined.
>   1422–8

13

We should not need the Chorus of *Henry V* to remind us how successfully Shakespeare's poetry appeals to the 'eye of mind' that willingly translates the shorthand of imaginative reference into the extended substance of reality. He and this 'painter' work to the same principles. The setting and subject-matter must be vast, with figures in a turmoil of excited movement, galvanised by every kind of human passion—alarm, envy, arrogance, hatred, ambition, despair. Behind the convulsions of interlocked armies and the smoke of burning cities, the artist hints at the steady drive of events towards their destined climax, in the death of a great leader and the overthrow of his country. The foreground is filled with individual human figures, caught in typical postures; sharply observed and portrayed with unerring judgement of the inward nature revealed by expression and mannerism:

> In Ajax and Ulysses, O what art
> Of physiognomy might one behold:
> The face of either cyphered either's heart;
> Their face their manners most expressly told.
> In Ajax' eyes blunt rage and rigour rolled,
> > But the mild glance that sly Ulysses lent
> > Showed deep regard and smiling government.
>
> > > 1394–1400

It is not to the point that the dramatist uses another means of disclosing individual nature: what must interest us is Shakespeare's assumption that a discerning knowledge of human character is vital to heroic art. The contrast between blunt Ajax and sly Ulysses is obvious enough, but here as in the other portraits—of grave Nestor, wrinkled Hecuba, innocent-seeming Sinon—Shakespeare is displaying a charged awareness of character and temperament which his dramatic writing will develop more subtly. His respect for the painter's expert knowledge of physiognomy, which sees in Ulysses' 'mild glance' an index of confident mastery, admits the standard of portraiture in depth which Shakespeare himself adopts, making his characters unconsciously reveal their private natures through speech, as the painter's figures through facial expressions. Because the whole painting is shaped by the same imaginative impulse as forms the plays, and so far as differences of medium allow expressed in the same terms, it represents Shakespeare's world of imagination at the time of the early history-plays.

The tumultuousness that characterises *Henry VI* is strongly evident, not only in the press of struggling figures but in the disorganisation of the whole picture. Its panorama has no central figure or scene. It is made up of snatches of action torn from some greater work and assembled arbitrarily, its confusion heightened by the barely controlled vitality of these individual fragments. Nestor exhorts a disordered mob whose angry energies are with difficulty held in restraint by his persuasive rhetoric:

> Here one being throng'd bears back, all boll'n and red;
> Another, smothered, seems to pelt and swear;
> And in their rage such signs of rage they bear
>   As, but for loss of Nestor's golden words,
>   It seemed they would debate with angry swords.
>
> 1417–21

The passage introduces the concept of rule, and suggests the dangerous force of the popular body upon which the monarch must impose his authority. By controlling the mob, Nestor seems to represent the poet's competence to direct the vital impulses of his art; but the disordered triumph of passion and destructive energy depicted throughout the painting leaves this mastery in some doubt. The undirected drive of the picture is finally contained only by its frame: the domestic interior which encloses the raw violence shared by Lucrece, the spectator and critic who is also participant in all that the picture represents.

The picture gives form to Shakespeare's sense of history. The fall of Troy is to be regarded as a momentous historical event, and the opposing generals and warriors as great historical figures. But the idea of history represented in Lucrece's compendious painting is not an impersonal, preordained movement of fate in which men are involved as subservient pigmies. It is the immediate outcome of human passions, asserting themselves blindly and forcing issues to a rapid outcome, with no thought of its eventual effect upon a larger design of developments. The figures which Lucrece studies derive their character from the driving emotions which dominate their whole outlook. Their passions impel them to act for good or bad, and their actions determine the events which make up the course of history, as Sinon's deceit and Priam's trustfulness help to produce the fall of Troy. History—in this context a compound of domestic and political disaster, of upheaval and overthrow, bloodshed and rapine—is the ultimate consequence of man's susceptibility to the impulses of his passionate being. To reveal the diversity of emotional impulse and its irresistible force is a concern which Shakespeare shares with the painter of Lucrece's picture. This must be reckoned among the major purposes of the early Histories.

This purpose is associated with the creative activity which Lucrece observes in the vigorously lifelike details of the artist's work. The digression from her private story to the Trojan War suddenly throws the poem open. It introduces an epic theme, a mass of human figures, and the portentous issues of a great historical epoch to over-shadow her private tragedy; and it turns attention upon the creative power of the artist, fulfilled only in a work of this heroic scale. Shakespeare might be giving notice of a disinclination to restrict himself to simply domestic themes, however sensational. His imagination is clamour-ing for a grander and more ambitious subject on which to prove its abundant creative energy, by filling cities with men, deploying armies and fleets, and showing the course of rebellion and war. Only one subject offered scope enough:

> Suppose within the girdle of these walls
> Are now confined two mighty monarchies,
> Whose high upreared and abutting fronts
> The perilous narrow ocean parts asunder . . .
> Into a thousand parts divide one man,
> And make imaginary puissance . . .
> Turning the accomplishment of many years
> Into an hour-glass.
>
> *Henry V*, i. 19-31

However it may have developed later, Shakespeare's early interest in history was not activated by a sense of moral retribution working itself out through political disorder and bloodshed. Upheaval and disquiet form a leading theme of the Histories because these conditions match Shakespeare's awareness of the driving energies impelling growth and change, in political affairs as in the world of natural life. In its concern with the decisive events of human destiny, and the thrusting ambitions and passions that brought them about, history gave Shakespeare the only matter that could absorb his giant energies at the beginning of his career.

An imaginative view of life does not necessarily exclude moral awareness, but homiletic commentary on the events of history is alien to Shakespeare's creative purpose. So far as it is valid to speak of his moral outlook, its conditions are those formed by the action and interests of the play, and not added to it from outside. *Macbeth* itself brings into being the particular standards by which the protagonist is to be judged, and which help to form the world of the play. The audience makes Macbeth's moral discovery with him, as part of the complex experience which it undergoes during the performance; and does not learn by example that crime A must be followed by consequence B. Any moral conclusions drawn from the play relate to the world and the figures created by the poet, and only incidentally to the happenings of actual life. Although *Macbeth* enacts the moral truth that man is harmed by the evil he commits, this finding is meaningful only within the context which makes it imaginatively true; that is, the play. The same applies to the moral outlook of the Histories.

Belief that the history-plays act out the moral argument of the Homilies has encouraged an assumption that eight of the plays form tetralogies, to be read as a continuous work showing the evil consequences of deposing Richard II, which were to trouble England for the next eighty years. This view of the Histories is open to several objections. The most obvious is that their order of composition suggests no such purpose. Had Shakespeare intended from the outset to make the crime of deposing a lawful king responsible for all the disorder and havoc which the two tetralogies depict, he would hardly have chosen to begin his series with *Henry VI*, historically the midpoint of the whole timespan which his plays cover. If the moral theme entered his purposes when he began to write the so-called second tetralogy, *Henry VI* and *Richard III* cannot be claimed as part of an extended moral commentary. The first four Histories have their own imaginative *raison d'être*, and are unlikely to share a common purpose with a group of plays written at a later point of Shakespeare's development. It is more reasonable to suppose that if the Histories contain some collective meaning, it is compatible with their order of composition.

But to believe that a close imaginative association could exist between plays separated by an interval of some years is not easy. Shakespeare's development as a poet was unusually rapid. Between *Henry VI* and *Henry IV* the power and fluency of his writing increase steadily, keeping pace with the deepening imaginative insight which accompanies and modifies his field of dramatic interest. Familiar themes and points of attention persist, changed by repeated handling which refashions and realigns them. No aspect of his writing is constant, for in the process of realising imaginative concepts through writing a play Shakespeare shifts his position, and brings himself to a fresh starting-point. That so organic a creative process should have a fixed centre in a moral view of history which Shakespeare pursued for eight years seems inconceivable. To see a single purpose running unchanged through eight plays we must disregard the essentially poetic character of his work.

Objection to the moral interpretation of the Histories does not rest on general arguments alone. We are entitled to ask what indications of Shakespeare's moral purpose are to be found in the earlier tetralogy; especially in backward references to the crime committed by Bolingbroke, from which 'disorder, horror, fear and mutiny' were to spring. *Henry VI*, with its endless turmoil and carnage, could be held to represent the fulfilling of Carlisle's prophecy. But, setting aside the fact that all Shakespeare's history-plays are concerned with political disorder, there is no evidence in *Henry VI* that at that time Shakespeare recognised any special significance in Bolingbroke's crime. Throughout this first history-play the deposition of Richard is spoken of simply as a political event, whose importance lies in its bearing upon the claims and counter-claims of the Yorkist struggle. Bolingbroke's interruption of the royal line deprived Richard's chosen heir of his inheritance, and gave the crown to a house whose authority was to be questioned by repeated uprisings against the Lancastrian kings. Richard is mentioned only as the starting-point of this interminable conflict. The circumstances of his deposition are related as plain historical facts, without overtones of moral condemnation. Mortimer, as Richard's intended successor hardly an impartial witness, recalls the usurpation simply as an event of past history:

> Henry the Fourth, grandfather to this king,
> Deposed his nephew Richard, Edward's son,
> The first begotten and the lawful heir
> Of Edward King, the third of that descent.
> > Pt. 1, ii. 5. 63–66

When York repeats the story in order to win Salisbury and Warwick to his cause, he shows more sense of the injustice of Bolingbroke's proceeding; but like Mortimer he makes no appeal to moral indignation, and does not suggest that the deposition was a crime for which England continues to suffer. 'The eldest son and heir of John of Gaunt,' he reminds his audience,

> Seized on the realm, deposed the rightful king,
> Sent his poor queen to France, from whence she came,
> And him to Pomfret; where, as all you know,
> Harmless Richard was murdered traitorously.
>
> Pt. 2, ii. 2. 23–26

York, it might be observed, is hardly the character to protest at Bolingbroke's contempt for the sanctity of the king. If his own cause is to prosper, he too must depose an anointed sovereign, breaking his oath of fealty and bringing bloodshed upon the kingdom. But we are concerned with Shakespeare's purposes, not with the motives he imputes to York. Had it been ironically presented, York's speech could have admitted the moral implications of the crime he intends to re-enact, with the same disregard of established law. The device is not used, and York's summary of past history offers no hint of a sacrilegious wrong committed two generations earlier. No character of *Henry VI* attempts to attribute the confusion and misery of civil war to the sin perpetrated by Bolingbroke. The disordered state of the kingdom derives chiefly from the failure of a weak-willed King to enforce his authority. The situation is accountable by circumstances which the action makes plain, and Shakespeare does not look towards the reading of historical events outlined by Carlisle in a play not yet written, and with which *Henry VI* would bear very little imaginative relationship.

The most important of the passages of *Henry VI* looking back to Richard's deposition occurs in the opening scene of Part 3, where the two claimants to the crown confront each other in a Parliament of armed men. After an exchange of taunts and insults, the King agrees to submit a reasoned defence of his right to the throne. His argument runs into difficulties at once:

> *King:* Henry the Fourth by conquest got the crown.
> *York:* 'Twas by rebellion against his king.
> *King:* I know not what to say; my title's weak.
>   Tell me, may not a king adopt an heir?
> *York:* What then?
> *King:* And if he may, then am I lawful king;
>   For Richard, in the view of many lords,
>   Resigned the crown to Henry the Fourth,
>   Whose heir my father was, and I am his.
> *York:* He rose against him, being his sovereign,
>   And made him to resign his crown perforce.
>
> Pt. 3, i. 1. 136–46

York's counter-argument is deeply ironic. He too wishes to possess the crown by rebelling against his King, compelling Henry to resign his authority as Richard had been forcibly deposed by Bolingbroke. The case which he brings against surrender of title under duress is to be ignored in this parallel instance, if York is successful. Again, although seeming to reject the contention that a king may lawfully adopt an heir, York accepts the compromise solution of allowing Henry to retain the crown until his death, when it will pass to York as due successor. His whole argument is not so much a repudiation of Bolingbroke's illegality as an oblique admission of the same political purpose, supported by the same cynical manipulation of moral standards to suit his private ends. Nothing could be further from a disinterested defence of Richard's stolen rights, or from a repudiation of Bolingbroke's half-forgotten crime. Like his characters, Shakespeare expresses no interest in the moral problems raised by Bolingbroke's succession. The deposition is treated as a political fact, not as an affront to divine will whose consequences are symbolised by an armed debate in Parliament. Shakespeare's attention is concentrated on the ironies of a situation in which the Yorkists, professing respect for justice and rightful inheritance, employ the same forms of moral casuistry as they condemn in their enemies, and try to secure the crown by exactly parallel means. Within this field of ironic duplication the importance of Richard is merely nominal.

Later in Part 3, during Warwick's embassy to France, the issue of Richard's deposition is raised once more. It enters unexpectedly. Seeking to prevent the marriage of the Lady Bona with Edward IV, Queen Margaret warns the French King not to depend upon the promises of a ruler whose authority is so doubtful, Henry and Prince Edward being still alive. 'Look therefore,' she advises Louis,

> Thou draw not on thy danger and dishonour;
> For though usurpers sway the rule awhile,
> Yet heavens are just, and time suppresseth wrongs.
>
> Pt. 3, iii. 3. 75–77

The usurper she refers to is Warwick's master, but Warwick picks up a deeper significance from her speech, and turns the warning back upon Margaret and her son:

> Thy father Henry did usurp,
> And thou no more art prince than she is queen.
>
> Ibid., 79, 80

This prompts Oxford to take up the defence of Henry's lineal right:

23

Then Warwick disannuls great John of Gaunt,
Which did subdue the greatest part of Spain;
And after John of Gaunt, Henry the Fourth,
Whose wisdom was a mirror to the wisest;
And, after that wise prince, Henry the Fifth,
Who by his prowess conquered all France:
From these our Henry lineally descends.

Ibid., 81–87

This does not answer the now familiar objection made by
Warwick, but by this stage of *Henry VI* it must be clear
that the moral issues of Richard's deposition figure only
as a political debating-point. The disordered world of the
play contains no representative of moral law capable of
challenging its debased standards, or of discriminating
between the self-interested claims of rival claimants to
the crown. Its only effective arguments are pragmatic. In
tracing Henry's descent from a son of Edward III,
Oxford demonstrates a respect for hard facts which
characterises both sides. Neither faction seems aware of
other forms of argument. The moral contentions put
forward by York are completely discredited by the
motives which he reveals in uttering them. The kind of
moral consciousness expressed by Carlisle before Richard's
deposition is not in evidence here. Richard himself is
mentioned only as a remote and uncharacterised figure,
relevant only by reason of the intercepted descent of title
willed to Edmund Mortimer. Nothing in *Henry VI*
encourages an assumption that this three-part play was
written to show the terrible consequences of deposing
God's deputy-elect.

The moral awareness of *Henry VI* lies elsewhere. The
charge that the usurping house of Lancaster has no title
to the crown is not treated seriously by either side, mere

legality counting for nothing among men who settle
disputed issues by main force. York has a more effective
argument in the innate authority which he enjoys and
Henry lacks. 'Thou art not king,' he tells his sovereign,

> Not fit to govern and rule multitudes,
> Which darest not, no, nor canst not rule a traitor . . .
> Here is a hand to hold a sceptre up,
> And with the same to act controlling laws.
> Give place: by heaven, thou shalt rule no more
> O'er him whom heaven created for thy ruler.
>
> Pt. 2, v. 1. 94–105

His claim involves moral contradictions which, although
unobserved by York, have a place in Shakespeare's
purposes. The speaker sees himself as king by natural
right, yet to prove Henry's impotence he admits himself
a traitor whom his appointed sovereign cannot put down.
The heaven which created York to be a ruler is not the
power acknowledged by Henry, 'whose far unworthy
deputy I am', but a savage natural impulse which drives
him to satisfy a craving for personal magnificence, at
whatever cost. The King himself is a figure of paradox, a
possessor of the crown whose perverse ambition is to
become a commoner:

> Was never subject longed to be a king
> As I do long and wish to be a subject.
>
> Pt. 2, iv. 9. 5–6

The paradox is inverted in a succession of subjects
burning with impatience to be king, for whom life can
only justify itself when it is linked with supreme power.
'Steel thy fearful thoughts,' York encourages himself,

> Be that thou hop'st to be, or what thou art
> Resign to death; it is not worth th'enjoying.
>
> Pt. 2, iii. 1. 333–4

His assertion that he deserves the crown by virtue of his soaring pride and energy would be accepted even by some of Henry's supporters, who are exasperated by the King's unmanly tameness. When Queen Margaret voices her incredulous feelings,

> Enforced thee? Art thou king, and wilt be forced?
>
> Pt. 3, i. 1. 237

she reveals a conception of kingly majesty which only Henry himself does not respect. The King should prove his title not by wise government, personal sanctity or concern for his people, but by a display of unchallenged power. Henry, who begins by abjectly surrendering France, who disinherits his son in favour of an impudent rebel, who allows himself to be silenced and driven from the battlefield by his own supporters, cannot claim to personate this figure. York shows a more appropriate respect for the awesome power of kingship:

> That gold must round engirt these brows of mine,
> Whose smile and frown, like to Achilles' spear,
> Is able with the change to kill and cure.
>
> Pt. 2, v. 1. 99–101

Like the claim through ancestral right, this conception of royal authority is supported by an irresistible urge towards personal power, which uses the forms of moral law only to disguise its true nature. In common with other aspirants to supreme power, York is driven by a consuming and unreasoning passion which cares nothing for the legal arguments in his favour. They follow, and do not motivate his attempt to seize the crown. From the beginning he is dazzled by a prospect which makes him contemptuous of restraint and caution, and regardless of moral law. Some part of his mind seems to recognise that he is possessed by a frenzy that will destroy him; for he com-

ments that the nobles who provide him with troops for
his Irish campaign have 'put sharp weapons in a madman's hands'; but the ironic truth of the comparison
escapes him. He sees himself as a man infuriated by the
frustration of personal energies which can only fulfil
themselves in kingship:

> This fell tempest shall not cease to rage
> Until the golden circuit on my head,
> Like to the glorious sun's transparent beams,
> Do calm the fury of this mad-bred flaw.
>
> Pt. 2, iii. 1. 351–4

His ambition is a madness that blinds him to hazards,
that induces him to gamble life, honour and possessions
on the outcome of a reckless throw, and which will
eventually destroy him. His insane venture ends in an
insulting parody of the magnificence which he thought to
possess. Helplessly pinioned, invested with a makeshift
crown and ceremoniously mocked by his murderous
captors, he discovers the emptiness of the kingly illusion
for which he has ruined himself. His sons are not warned
by this tragic example. Unlike his father, Clarence
recognises that the lure of kingly power and majesty
maddens its victims with a self-destructive fury; but he
refuses to be deterred by the suicidal risks of continuing
the struggle. 'We set the axe to thy usurping root,' he
tells Queen Margaret before the battle of York,

> And though the edge hath something hit ourselves,
> Yet know thou, since we have begun to strike,
> We'll never leave till we have hewn thee down,
> Or bathed thy growing with our heated bloods.
>
> Pt. 3, ii. 2. 166–9

His brother Richard, obsessed by the same senseless
ambition, is twisted out of shape by a compulsion that

destroys all peace of mind and drains him of human
sympathies. Like York, he is tormented by a frustrated
appetite for absolute power, feeling himself in hell

> Until my misshaped trunk that bears this head
> Be round impaled with a glorious crown.
>
> Pt. 3, iii. 2. 170–1

He knows what hurt he must inflict upon himself in
forcing a path through lacerating obstacles towards his
goal; and accepts the hazards like a man drugged or
brutalised into insensibility. His soliloquy, one of the
earliest passages of imaginative self-disclosure in the
plays, reveals Richard's helpless inability to control his
lust for power, and the frenzy of mind which drives him
towards the satisfaction of a tormenting desire:

> Like one lost in a thorny wood,
> That rents the thorns, and is rent with the thorns;
> Seeking a way, and straying from the way,
> Not knowing how to find the open air,
> But toiling desperately to find it out,
> Torment myself to catch the English crown.
>
> Ibid., 174–9

His cruelty to others reflects the inward anguish of a
nature wrenched out of true by a compulsion too overwhelming to be mastered. As he struggles to break out
of the restraints that thwart his will to power, gashing and
impaling himself upon the disregarded curbs which goad
him forward, he becomes increasingly benighted. When,
at the end of this soliloquy, he recalls himself from bewilderment in a sudden outburst of resolution,

> And from that torment I will free myself,
> Or hew my way out with a bloody axe
>
> Ibid., 180–1

he admits his helplessness to act except through the violence which must destroy his own being. The thorny wood in which he is lost is the nightmarish world of his own monstrously distorted and protesting humanity.

Richard's soliloquy, and the related speeches of York and Clarence, help to resolve the moral viewpoint from which Shakespeare presents the behaviour of these allied figures. Each of them is torn between an instinctive drive towards self-fulfilment in political power and an awareness of obligations to moral law which cannot be crushed without fatally injuring man's implanted nature. Shakespeare's awareness of the driving energies which moral respect should contain is obviously very keen. His imaginative concern with the sheerly brutish impulses which impel man to repudiate the restraints of moral law is unmistakably declared in *Lucrece*, and becomes a persistent motif of Shakespearean history. In *Henry VI* York rejects the restraints of loyalty and subordination which safeguard society, claiming allegiance for himself in contempt of established order. His insanely selfish ambition throws the kingdom into confusion; but this triumph of private will over reason and moral conscience has consequences for York that are no less disastrous. Like his son Richard, whose misshapen body and wolfish isolation characterise the ugly impulses which moral law should subdue, York inflicts fatal injury upon himself by outraging the respects by which humanity is nourished. Man's moral consciousness, Shakespeare implies, cannot be tied off if the individual is to survive. His instinctive desire for society and friendship, and for the deeper satisfactions of true allegiance, faithful service and ordered prerogative, spring from an implanted impulse that is vital to his existence as a man. When he repudiates

29

this impulse, letting private will determine his behaviour, he cuts himself off from rational judgement and self-knowledge, and becomes a madman blundering through the labyrinth of his own passions, more confused at every step.

Such a moral positive is stated early in the trilogy of *Henry VI*, in the only scene of the play to provide a retrospective link with the events of Richard II's reign. Edmund Mortimer, named by the childless Richard as his heir, and subsequently held a lifelong prisoner by three Lancastrian kings, makes his single appearance in the second act of Part 1; a blind and broken figure who dies in prison after wishing prosperity to York. He has a dramatic function of some importance. From him the Yorkist cause derives its decisive initial impulse, when Mortimer describes in detail how he and his descendants have been forcibly disinherited by Bolingbroke, and then exhorts his kinsman to recover the title wrongfully held by the usurper's grandson. The upheaval of civil war treated in the two later parts of *Henry VI* and in *Richard III* is seen to draw its original impulse from Mortimer in this scene, where frustrated ambition is passed down to a youthful successor, eager to renew an almost extinguished claim to the crown.

As the tragic relic of an insurrection ruthlessly crushed by Bolingbroke nearly thirty years earlier, Mortimer symbolises the tragic emptiness of the ambition which has wasted the vitality and promise of his own youth. In a play whose action is dominated by a series of attempts to snatch the crown, he is the first representative of the lust for power which impels them all; but Mortimer's attempt is long past, and the figure who communicates the same deadly impulse to York embodies the futility of all such aspirations. Emaciated, sightless and physically impotent after a lifetime of imprisonment, he is blind to his own example, and cannot warn York against the waste of life and substance that his pursuit of the crown has entailed; nor can York appreciate the moral lesson which confronts him. When he asks Mortimer to explain how his father came to be executed, Mortimer replies imperceptively:

> That cause, fair nephew, that imprisoned me,
> And hath detained me all my flowering youth
> Within a loathsome dungeon, there to pine,
> Was cursed instrument of his decease.
>
> Pt. 1, ii. 5. 55–58

York seeks a more detailed account of events from the deposition of Richard II, remarking simply, 'For I am ignorant, and cannot guess'; and Mortimer describes the struggle against Bolingbroke without acknowledging the blindness he shares with York. Uncle, father and son are victims of the same insane impulse, which obliterates all sense of personal danger and moral obligation by its promise of majesty and unbounded power. At the end of the scene, death puts an end to Mortimer's exhausted and delusive hopes of achieving the crown. To York this final extinction of hope indicates only a want of lofty aspiration in Mortimer. 'Here dies the dusky torch of Mortimer,' he comments over his uncle's body, 'Choked with ambition of the meaner sort.' His own end at the hands of Clifford and Queen Margaret will be still more ignominious, and will provide a more emphatic comment on the deadly consequences of disclaiming the authority of moral consciousness in man.

For men of such ruthless energy and will the doubtfulness of Henry's title is not a serious issue. Their conception of kingship as the most glorious of prizes—'Ah, *sancta Majestas*! who would not buy thee dear?'—makes them impatient and contemptuous of Henry's unmanly dislike of force, and of his refusal to assert the kingly power which they covet. None of the disaffected nobles recognises that Henry possesses some of the vital qualities of a king, which the savagery of the times discredits. Before the battle of Barnet Henry himself enumerates the gentle virtues which should endear him to his people and assure their allegiance:

> My pity hath been balm to heal their wounds,
> My mildness hath allayed their swelling griefs,
> My mercy dried their water-flowing tears.
>
> Pt. 3, iv. 8. 41–43

By assuming that the commons will support him out of respect for his humanity Henry shows himself out of touch with political reality, but he is right to think that these kindly qualities befit a king. His nobles do not contest the claim he makes for himself. 'Your grace hath still been famed for virtuous,' Warwick encourages him; and the Yorkists, whose main effort is directed against Henry's entourage rather than against their incapable figurehead, describe him more than once as 'the gentle king'. His anguish of spirit over the horrors of civil war expresses a genuine concern for the well-being of his people and realm which is shared by none of the savage aspirants to power. By attempting to act as peacemaker between enraged nobles whom only brute force would silence he shows himself naïvely trustful and simple. His gentle spirit cannot reconcile itself with the sterner responsibilities of kingship, and by failing to act resolutely in defence of his own authority he allows his strength to be whittled away, and weakens all force of law throughout his kingdom. Queen Margaret analyses him justly:

> Henry, my lord, is cold in great affairs;
> Too full of foolish pity.
>
> Pt. 2, iii. 1. 224–5

Clifford urges him to rid himself of the charitable impulse which hampers the royal party's conduct of the war:

> My gracious liege, this too much lenity
> And harmful pity must be laid aside.
>
> Pt. 3, ii. 2. 9f.

The practical argument for acting rigorously against ruthless opponents has obvious force; but in their contempt for pity, stigmatised as foolish and harmful, both Clifford and the Queen are motivated by a vicious cruelty of nature, and not by simply political considerations. The murder of the boy Rutland by Clifford, and Queen Margaret's part in the taunting and stabbing of their captive York, show a sadistic inhumanity of purpose which has nothing to do with the strong-minded direction of war. Clifford mocks Rutland's plea for pity with a cynical promise, 'Such pity as my rapier's point affords'; and although Northumberland is moved almost to tears by York's outburst of grief for his murdered son, the Queen outrages the standards of womanly softness and compassion by exulting over his misery. As she stabs York 'to right our gentlehearted king', her own epithet condemns her, and suggests how little relationship exists between Henry and his barbarous protectors. The crime proves an association of kind between Queen Margaret and the King's murderer, who poniards his defenceless victim with the same contempt for humanity and moral law. Henry's dying words to Richard,

c

33

O God forgive my sins, and pardon thee
Pt. 3, v. 6. 60

are true to the piety and gentleness which characterise
him throughout the play: qualities which his age regards
as incompatible with the exercise of kingly authority.
Compassion, kindness and mercy are flung aside by the
forces of animal energy that admit no restraint upon their
pursuit of self-fulfilment through power.

The brutality, violence and moral obliviousness that
typify political ambition in the early-history plays are
most fully embodied in the deformed figure of Richard of
Gloucester. Ugly, hated, and proud of his moral repulsive-
ness, he repudiates all claims of kinship and affection
which might weaken his determination to hack out a
path to the crown. 'I have no brother,' he affirms,

> I am like no brother;
> And this word 'love', which greybeards call divine,
> Be resident in men like one another,
> And not in me: I am myself alone.
>
> Ibid., 80–83

He sees his isolation as a personal triumph over the
affections which soften other men; but in fact it represents
a perversion of the instinct which makes man a social
creature who relies upon the environment of family and
society to realise his implanted nature. By dissociating
himself from human ties Richard displays a monstrous-
ness of character in keeping with his warped and stunted
body: he is not more but less than other men. Modern
psychology may see his sadistic cruelty and appetite for
power as a consequence of the physical deformity which
constantly humiliates him. Shakespeare probably intended
his ugliness to reflect his misshapen moral nature, as a

man whose rapacious animal will has smothered all sense
of kindly relationship. It is imaginatively and dramatically
appropriate that Richard should strike down the now
saintly King, destroying the figure of gentle humanity
which stands as a rebuke to his brutishness. The crime
has a strongly emblematic quality. It brings together on
the stage, alone, characters who personify the warring
houses of Lancaster and York; and who also embody the
moral polarity between kindliness and ferocity, restraint
and lawlessness, which underlies the action of *Henry VI*
as a persistent theme of attention. To interpret this
scene—whose moral and dramatic issues bear closely
upon Shakespeare's imaginative purposes—on simply
political lines would be to ignore its poetic significance.
The outraging of helpless innocence by blindly passionate
will is a major theme of Shakespeare's work, realised in
the simplest and most potent terms in *The Rape of
Lucrece*. At a much later point of Shakespeare's career the
same theme, its basic form unchanged, provides the
central event of *Macbeth;* where the murdered King who
'hath borne his faculties so meek' bears a suggestive
likeness to the pious and gentle-hearted figure butchered
by Richard in *Henry VI*. In none of these three works does
Shakespeare seem interested in developing the story along
moralistic lines, to show the eventual punishment of
crime: rather, he is concerned with an insistent imaginative figure whose meaning must be sought in the terms
through which it finds expression.

In *Lucrece* this recurrent figure is epitomised in the
violation of a virtuous and unprotected woman by the
man whom she has received as a guest. Like other victims
of brutal violence in the plays, Lucrece stands in a relationship to her wrongdoer which should assure her safety, but

she is betrayed from within. In *Macbeth* the condition is reversed: the host who should defend Duncan bears the knife that murders him; but in both works victim and agent of violence are associated in an equivocal relationship which makes the crime self-destructive; an act directed against an attribute of the doer which cannot protect itself. The saintly king whom Macbeth butchers personifies the element of moral respect in his own nature which Macbeth deliberately outrages. Such an underlying significance would account for the unusual degree of imaginative engagement felt in Shakespeare's treatment of a dramatic theme which symbolises the sudden and irrevocable collapse of moral authority in the individual. It is the prospect of this ultimate horror which gives force to the threat uttered against the citizens of Harfleur:

> Why, in a moment look to see
> The blind and bloody soldier, with foul hand
> Defile the locks of your shrill-shrieking daughters;
> Your fathers taken by the silver beards,
> And their most reverend heads dashed to the walls;
> Your naked infants spitted upon pikes,
> Whiles the mad mothers, with their howls confused,
> Do break the clouds as did the wives of Jewry
> At Herod's bloody-hunting slaughtermen.
>
> *Henry V*, iii, 3. 33–41

This speech is less readily associated with its noble speaker than with the poet, whose dialogue is under pressure from a theme of great imaginative power. It might be possible to justify the King's threat to unleash carnage upon a civilian population; but the peculiar energy of the speech is not accountable simply by reference to the speaker's supposed character. An obsessive idea has broken into the play: the violation of a helpless community by a mob of frenzied brutes who 'in a moment' will transform a peaceful town into a shambles. For this not the King but Shakespeare is responsible. There is more incompatibility of character in the King's warning that, once licensed to rape and slaughter, his soldiers cannot be recalled to good discipline. 'What is't to me,' he asks callously,

> If your pure maidens fall into the hand
> Of hot and forcing violation?
> What rein can hold licentious wickedness
> When down the hill he holds his fierce career?
>
> Ibid., 20–23

Yet later, 'When lenity and cruelty play for a kingdom,' he will remark, 'the gentler gamester is the soonest winner.' An attempt to reconcile these conflicting attitudes would imply some misunderstanding of the nature of Shakespeare's work. Speeches are not directed exclusively by the poet's conception of the speaker's individuality. In the history-plays especially, the subject-matter encourages Shakespeare to develop ideas of physical violence, rapine and bloodshed, reflecting an imaginative turbulence which does not always match the emotional temper of the speaker. If we are determined to regard Henry V as an ideal king we shall disregard his admission that, once the city has been stormed, he will be unable to restrain his 'blind and bloody' troops; interpreting the threat as a bluff. His army is a submissive instrument of war, acting as a disciplined force under the King's will.

The creative energy of the speech denies this. Readings based on character or the art of rhetoric cannot neutralise the imaginative effect of writing so positive in its suggestions of havoc and brutality. The ferocious images have their own truth, which cannot be explained out of

37

existence. The King is not absolute master of the destructive forces which he is leading to war. Once the headstrong fury of his 'bloody-hunting slaughtermen' is
released, he will be unable to reimpose restraint upon it.
His insistence, later in the play, upon the moral discipline
of his army, that 'there be nothing compelled from the
villages; nothing taken but paid for', shows his determination to hold disorder and savagery in check. The potential
danger remains.

It may not be possible to understand the full significance of the speech before Harfleur without taking other
Histories into consideration. In all of them the efforts of a
king to impose his authority upon an unruly kingdom, or
to resist the challenge of open rebellion, is a matter of
first account. The persistence of this subject, from *Henry
VI* onwards, has been the main support of interpretations
based upon the political morality of the Homilies, and
of the argument that the two tetralogies show the consequences of lifting hands against God's deputy. If, instead, we assume that Shakespeare used the matter of the
English chronicles for an essentially imaginative purpose,
the repeated—and generally unsuccessful—attempts of a
king to assert his authority over rebellious subjects take
on a very different appearance. It now becomes a point of
imaginative significance that none of the six kings in these
eight plays enjoys an undisputed title to the crown, and
must fight to retain it. The first of Shakespeare's sover-
eigns, 'in infant bands crowned king', is the weakest
and least effectual in resisting the challenge to his title
and possession; the last the strongest and most assured of
his legitimacy. This development running through the
Histories, by which the king acquires an increasing force
of authority, shows why it must be mistaken to treat the

series as though it were intended to begin with the deposition of Richard and to end with the accession of Henry Tudor. The historical order of the six reigns is not relevant to Shakespeare's imaginative purpose: the chronological order of the plays is. The historical matter is treated in a sequence which illustrates that purpose; beginning at the point of greatest political confusion and national weakness, with a king incapable of ruling his insubordinate subjects, and ending after a great victory by the only English monarch whom Shakespeare presents as a national hero.

Throughout the series the king, whether usurper or rightful heir, sits uneasily on his throne; under assault from rivals whose ambition he must contain if he is not to lose his crown. His task is one of personal domination; to prove himself king by mastering the rebellious factions that deny his authority and threaten to unseat him. In Henry VI Shakespeare depicts a king whose gentle nature is appalled by the savagery of political conflict, and who cannot face the necessity of forcing obedience upon the mutinous nobles whom his own weakness has encouraged. Their unruly energy can only be held in balance by an equally resolved force impressing order upon them, but the King evades his obligation in the pious hope that mild persuasion will prove an effective substitute for political mastery. Held in contempt by both sides, he is thrust outside the arena of political decisions, a king only in his own thoughts; having lost all influence upon the government of his disordered kingdom.

Despite obvious differences of character and situation, the collapse of discipline and moral restraint which Henry V describes to the citizens of Harfleur bears a close imaginative relationship to the disasters which

39

follow Henry VI's failure to assert his sovereignty. The savagery which the King threatens to let loose represents the transformed character of a disciplined army which has slipped the leash of humanity and civilised respect. The analogy with the rape of Lucrece again offers itself as the seminal type of this Shakespearean theme, as much in respect of the brutalised Tarquin as of his gentle victim. The consequences of a breakdown of moral authority in *Henry VI* are as frightful as the indiscriminate carnage promised to the citizens of Harfleur. In both a rush of passionately inflamed impulse which the King cannot control sweeps away all moral restraint and throws society into a turmoil of bloodshed and terror. To conclude that kings must enforce their authority or be overwhelmed, or that humane government must be supported by resolute action, might seem an acceptable response to *Henry VI*; but these conclusions have no relevance to the central situation of *The Rape of Lucrece*, whose imaginative association with the play is very marked. They are also without bearing on the warning to Harfleur, which expresses the same thematic ideas in a different form.

The situation asks to be seen as a metaphor, whose key is provided by a stanza from the climax of the poem. In Lucrece's bedchamber, Tarquin's unlawful passions are about to take possession of him:

> And they, like straggling slaves for pillage fighting,
> Obdurate vassals, fell exploits effecting,
> In bloody death and ravishment delighting,
> Nor children's tears nor mother's groans respecting,
> Swell in their pride, the onset still expecting:
>   Anon his beating heart, alarum striking,
>   Gives the hot charge, and bids them do their liking.

428–34

The stanza provides a gloss on some important features of the Harfleur speech, which exploits the same ideas within a dramatic situation, where the metaphor can be realised in literal terms without losing its moral significance. The 'obdurate vassals' of lust and fury take more particular form as the mob that will sack and ravish Harfleur, given its head by a commander who previously has kept its lawless brutality under restraint. The metaphor used in *Lucrece* carries its sense into the King's speech. The act of licensing rape and carnage will represent a rejection of moral respect by the King himself, throwing his rational being into an uproar from which he will have no power to recall himself.

It appears from this that Shakespeare's history-plays have an imaginative basis in metaphors of moral conflict within the individual. The earliest of these plays in particular reveal a charged awareness of the savagery of man's natural being, and of the limited ability of moral law to hold its destructive energies in check. In York, Clifford, Jack Cade and Richard of Gloucester the monster of natural instinct is at large and without a master, throwing society into disorder by uprooting its humane institutions. This theme provides the ground-work of Shakespeare's first four plays. The fact that their dramatic substance is taken from the English chronicles does not mean that their imaginative interest is centred upon historical events: rather, these events stand in the same relationship to Shakespeare's creative design as do the ravaging troops of passion to Tarquin's uncontrolled lust. It is in this sense that we may speak of the plays as extended metaphors, acting out an imaginative awareness of states and happenings whose nature they represent analogically. This need not imply that the Histories are open only to poetic interpretation; but their commentary on man's political behaviour or the shaping forces of history is of secondary importance. Their fullest significance is creative, and lies in the particular imaginative experience which they enact.

The early history-plays are thus seen to be directed by a close concern with man's moral identity; a fully adult interest which already dominates Shakespeare's outlook. *Henry VI* and *Richard III* realise on a much grander scale the overwhelming of rational restraint by savagery which the rape of Lucrece illustrates in the starkest of terms. In the poem the storming of Tarquin's civilised respect by lust is directly analogous to his violation of the helpless Lucrece, and the physical event again stands in the relationship of metaphor to the moral collapse which it represents. Conscious allegory is not involved, but an imaginative merging of purposes within the form of dramatic which makes its central event both an incident from Roman domestic history and a metaphor of conflict within the moral being of man. The two meanings are co-present aspects of the imaginative experience which *The Rape of Lucrece* is in the most generous sense 'about'.

These recurrent images of moral conflict may also be the means by which Shakespeare represents the tensions which accompany his own creative development. Much of his early work exhibits a curious dichotomy between style and matter, where the brutality and violence so prominent in the action are offset by a stiffly mannered literary style, often overloaded with artifice. Incongruous associations of the grim and the pretty persist as late as *Henry V*, where the deaths of York and Suffolk in battle are given courtly charm by Exeter's description. Such

writing might be expected of a young poet whose style
was much more consciously developed than his still
raw sense of drama; but the contrast between headstrong
energy and cultivated feeling in his work at this period is
more suggestive of an imaginative polarity. The driving
motives of his historical characters, whose hates, lusts,
and drunken ambitions seek to overthrow established
rule, embody forces which have a counterpart in Shakespeare himself. His creative energy is no less impulsive,
and finds an appropriate outlet in the dramatic images of
bloodshed and havoc which give the early Histories their
sensational character. The poet is committed to a subject
which enables him to realise the impetuous force of
creative energy put into his charge.

Like other arts, poetry depends not only upon the
creative potential of its maker, but upon the discipline
that imposes formal design upon this natural force. The
conspicuous element of artifice in Shakespeare's early
work is a measure of his creative energy; a curb proportionate to the imaginative drive which gives his poetry
its life. The striking contrast between barbarous behaviour
and a mannered formality of speech seems to reflect such a
conflict of impulse in Shakespeare's work, where the
disciplines of rhetoric struggle to contain an abundant
poetic vitality. The disparity is especially marked in
Lucrece, whose elaborately courtly style seems almost
perversely misapplied to subject-matter comprising lust,
betrayal, rape and suicide. The incongruity may be
deliberate and wanton. But Shakespeare's early development suggests that he was writing under pressure of
ideas which found most appropriate expression in images
of elemental violence, and that the overstressed urbanity
of his style represents an attempt to restrain his turbulent

imaginative energy. We should not suppose that the effort was unsuccessful; rather, that the lurid matter of the early Histories reflects Shakespeare's awareness of the dynamic force which his art was to tame. Yet the weakness of the king, or the doubtfulness of his authority, throughout all the plays of the two tetralogies except the last, is a feature of these Histories which asks to be explained.

In work as deeply imaginative as Shakespeare's, the significance of the king cannot be limited to his obvious political functions as ruler, supreme authority and deputy-elect. We cannot suppose that Shakespeare's kings begin as historical figures, and acquire imaginative depth through the associations which the poet develops about them. In the context of poetry, the king is an archetypal image invested with powerful associations which owe nothing to the chronicles. The ambitious nobles of *Henry VI* have a clear general concept of the qualities to which kingship and sovereignty give form: the majesty of absolute power, and the personal splendour of a crowned monarch. Richard II finds a still more imposing quality of kingship in the inviolable sanctity of his anointed person. The idea of the king which the plays themselves submit through their political speakers has far more bearing upon Shakespeare's purpose than contemporary Tudor assumptions about the nature of the sovereign and the duties of the subject. The world of the play and the world of contemporary life do not coincide, and Shakespeare is best to be understood by respecting the terms of imaginative reference which he employs. His idea of the king is not a political concept, and whether his royal figures are good or bad kings by Tudor standards is irrelevant. Shakespeare's king is an imaginative concept, developed from play to play, and keeping step with the growth of linked interests in his other plays of the period.

One of the most persistent of these interests, not confined to the early plays, is the issue of individual identity. We need not look so far forward as *King Lear*, and the King's question, 'Who is it that can tell me who I am?' for an indication of a particular link between Shakespeare's king and this crucial imaginative concern. The association is there from the first, expressed in simple form when York challenges the right of Henry VI to his title:

> King did I call thee? No, thou art not king;
> Not fit to govern and rule multitudes.
>
> Pt. 2, v. 1. 93–94

King is not merely a title but an identity, and in Henry the two do not coincide. The bare name of king demands to be supported by personal qualities, or its bearer makes a mockery of his great office; yet personal majesty without legal title falls short of what kingship should involve just as badly. Shakespeare's kings are a mixture of legal inheritors without natural title to the crown, and men of kingly ability debarred from true possession of the name they seize. The true inheritor put out of office becomes an anonymous figure, with neither royal title nor the identity of an individual man. When Henry is captured by the foresters after the battle of York he has been deposed by Edward IV, and cannot answer their question who he is:

King More than I seem, and less than I was born to;
      A man at least, for less I should not be;
      And men may talk of kings, and why not I?
2 Keep Ay, but thou talk'st as if thou wert a king.

King Why, so am I, in mind, and that's enough.
2 Keep But if thou be a king, where is thy crown?
Pt. 3, iii. 1. 56–61

The situation is developed without much subtlety, but Shakespeare is giving notice of an imaginative interest which will be pressed more firmly in plays still to come. In each of the later Histories the king is forced to come to terms with the nature of the royal identity which he has tried to assume, and to recognise a disparity between his ideal of majesty and his personal ability to fill the role assigned to him. The costume is laid out and the part rehearsed, but the performance falls short in respects which both actor and audience acknowledge. The player is not the king. However alluring in prospect, and however confidently the part is accepted, the task of realising this major role proves destructively taxing. The unachieved magnificence of the king finally appears to lie beyond human reach; a part which the actor relinquishes in the disillusioned spirit expressed by the poet of the Sonnets:

> Thus have I had thee as a dream doth flatter;
> In sleep a king, but waking no such matter.
> LXXXVII. 13–14

The remaining chapters of this book consider the attempts of the three later Shakespearean kings—Richard II, Henry Bolingbroke and Henry V—to assume the royal identity. The plays concerned are not treated simply as Histories, but as imaginative works whose interests run much deeper than the political issues which their action involves. The three figures are not approached as kings whose royal conduct invites judgement within a context of Elizabethan political ideas, but as men grappling with an identity bigger than their own; a form of human greatness which they try eagerly to substitute for the limitations of private name, which represents the known self. The problems of personal realisation which confront them have very little to do with English history, but very close affinity with an imaginative purpose which is seen developing throughout Shakespeare's work. The attempts of these three major figures to embody the royal identity in themselves do not possess the interest of a problem affecting humanity in general, nor does Shakespeare need this justification. The imaginative concerns of his plays relate to the world which the poet brings into existence, and not to the experiences of actual life. The task of self-identification, and the actor's struggle to become the part he plays, are issues which Shakespeare's creative consciousness never drops for long. In the later Histories they join to form a central theme of attention; using the image of king to embody the natural sovereignty which Renaissance man believed himself to possess, and the chronicler's records as a dramatic field where this exalted identity could be put to the test.

CHAPTER II

The Name of King

RICHARD II begins by declaring a concern with formal titles and modes of address which characterises the play. Its opening words, spoken to 'old John of Gaunt, time-honoured Lancaster', identify an important figure and also establish the curiously impersonal idiom of Richard's kingdom, where even gardeners speak in set rhetorical terms. This stilted mode of address suggests the addiction to ceremonial form which Richard seems to find natural whatever the circumstances: an appropriate concomitant of the personal majesty which he never allows himself to forget. As his subjects follow his example, little of the action of *Richard II* escapes from the formal atmosphere of public ceremony or kingly ritual. The range of emotions through which the King runs, from elation to tragic despair, is expressed in set terms which inhibit any show of spontaneous feeling: the dialogue is recited within a frame of predetermined response. Even when Richard bids farewell to the Queen there is a strange lack of *rapport* between the two, who speak as though listening to themselves; uttering declarations rather than conversing. This effect is evidently calculated. Richard lives on the surface of experience, denied contact with the inward reality of the self by his complete absorption in the identity of king, which he mistakes for it. The other characters of *Richard II* exist by virtue of their names and titles rather than as individual beings; and like him express themselves in prescribed forms and set rhetorical figures which mask direct personal response. The being of the man resides in his name.

The ritual of self-identification before the lists at Coventry, where appellant and defendant are required to declare themselves, has thus a wider significance within the play. The marshal's command, 'In God's name and the King's, say who thou art', suggests that the anonymous armed figures will give sufficient proof of their true identity simply by naming themselves. The defendant answers by giving his name and title:

> My name is Thomas Mowbray, Duke of Norfolk.
>
> i. 3. 16

and is followed by Bolingbroke, announcing himself as 'Harry of Hereford, Lancaster and Derby'. This public declaration of title is echoed several times by the heralds as both sides prepare for the combat that will test the 'foul traitor's name' applied to Mowbray. The formality of ancestral title covers more than disloyalty towards Richard in one of the combatants. The ceremony might have been devised to suppress all the personal traits which make up human character, and to oblige the participants to represent themselves by a bare name. Apart from their formal titles they are nothing.

Not only naming but the speaking of words assumes a significance in the opening scenes of *Richard II* which is justified by later developments, when the King repeatedly takes refuge from reality in verbal fantasy. Mowbray may object in the opening scene that his quarrel with Bolingbroke is too deadly to be settled by

> The bitter clamour of two eager tongues.
>
> i. 1. 49

but in fact their conflict does not progress beyond this exchange of spoken threats and insults. As Richard lives inside the illusion of majestic authority which his own speeches create, so the disputants are forced to accept angry speeches as a substitute for physical action. Bolingbroke is not allowed to prove 'what my tongue speaks' on the spot; and when later his accusation is about to be put to the test of combat, the King's intervention again frustrates his wish to give his words substance. The sentence of banishment passed upon Mowbray provides the motive for elaborations on the theme of speech— pronounce, word, breathe, mouth, language, tongue, teeth, lips, sentence, speechless—which make its utterance seem more momentous than the judgement itself. Mowbray's complaint implies that by preventing him from speaking his native language, Richard has condemned him to death. In terms of character this objection is hardly plausible, and the remark that

> Within my mouth you have engaoled my tongue
> Doubly portcullised with my teeth and lips.
>
> i. 3. 166f.

reveals an absorption in courtly conceit which any strong emotion would suppress. To account for the seeming triviality of Mowbray's reaction we must look beyond character to the purpose indicated by this concentration of interest on words and speech. Deprived of language, Mowbray will cease to exist. Fanciful in itself, his protest suggests the vital importance of words to the sense of actuality which they induce in a speaker who mistakes them for the objects they name.

Bolingbroke is quick to take advantage of the fact that man is not merely identified but represented by his name. At the death of Gaunt he returns from banishment with a new title, insisting that he must now be acknowledged as Lancaster, and that in this person he cannot be charged with Bolingbroke's act of treason. When Berkely innocently addresses him by his former title, Bolingbroke presses his legal quibble with some acerbity:

> My lord, my answer is, 'to Lancaster';
> For I am come to seek that name in England,
> And I must find that title in your tongue.
>
> ii. 3. 70–72

Berkeley apologises, explaining that he had not intended to 'raze one title of your honour out'. The disclaimer is needed, for during Bolingbroke's exile Richard and his followers have done their best to obliterate the name of Lancaster. Bolingbroke's impeachment of Bushy and Green includes an account of the personal indignities which he has suffered, and which have brought him back to England as a man without legal title to his family inheritance. 'You have fed upon my signories,' he accuses them,

> Disparked my parks and felled my forest woods;
> From my own windows torn my household coat,
> Razed out my impress, leaving me no sign . . .
> To show the world I am a gentleman.
>
> iii. 1. 23–27

The favourites have followed Richard's example, who seizes the whole of Lancaster's estate before Gaunt's breath is well out of his body. This brutal measure is motivated in part by the King's approaching bankruptcy, and triggered by the humiliation of Gaunt's dying rebuke; but during their final meeting Gaunt hints at a deeper personal motive of the King's animus towards the house of Lancaster. As he labours the macabre joke of a name that represents his physical condition, 'Gaunt am I for

the grave, gaunt as a grave,' Richard asks unsympathetic-
ally,

> Can sick men play so nicely with their names?
>
> ii. 1. 84

No, Gaunt replies, misery makes sport to mock itself; and
then, explaining his cryptic remark:

> Since thou dost seek to kill my name in me,
> I mock my name, great king, to flatter thee.
>
> ii. 1. 86–87

His misery stems from his son's banishment, which Gaunt
sees as an attempt first to destroy the father and then to
obstruct his heir's right of succession, so putting an end
to their house. After Gaunt's death, Bolingbroke finds
that he is debarred from inheriting both the title and the
ancestral property which should descend to him. As a
banished man, he is denied all form of legal redress against
these injuries. 'What would you have me do?' he asks
York with some evident reason;

> I am a subject,
> And I challenge law: attorneys are denied me,
> And therefore personally I lay my claim
> To my inheritance of free descent.
>
> ii. 3. 132–5

A man without name or property, he has been reduced to
the condition of a nobody, whose existence and common
rights the law refuses to acknowledge; and like the hero of
a later play he returns from banishment 'a kind of nothing,
titleless'.[1] The title of Lancaster is only part of the
inheritance which he comes for. Bolingbroke assures both
the King and his own supporters that he has returned
'but for mine own', but the phrase is calmly equivocal,
and includes what he can make his own as well as his legal

---

[1] *Coriolanus*, v. 1. 13

inheritance. As a banished man, he has been dispossessed by Richard—or in Ross's vigorous expression, gelded of his patrimony—and he may now seize Richard's inherited rights and title. During one of his phases of unrealistic confidence, Richard assures Aumerle that it will be simple to reassert his collapsed authority: 'An easy task it is to win our own.' What he assumes to be his unalienable property has already passed out of his hands. The name of king which he prizes will be won by the man who knows 'the strong'st and surest way to get', and who makes Richard's crown his own.

Richard's conception of his royal title and office is too lofty to admit the possibility that a rival might take over his function. He knows himself King by right of due succession and divine will, and is convinced that no earthly power can depose him. His belief that

> no hand of blood and bone
> Can gripe the sacred handle of our sceptre,
> Unless he do profane, steal, or usurp,
> iii. 3. 79–81

encourages him to ignore the approach of political disaster. His supporters watch him talking himself into a state of self-hypnotic assurance in which mere insistence upon his divinely protected authority becomes an acceptable substitute for purposeful action. Because he cannot divorce himself from the idea of kingly magnificence and sanctity, he habitually speaks of himself as an unearthly being whose trivial acts demand respectful attention. Himself the awed spectator of the royal performance, he is also the ecstatic commentator whose description clothes every action in the majesty which Richard claims for himself. His greeting to his kingdom when he returns from Ireland is characteristic of this self-admiring commentary, which supplies stage directions to his acting-out of royal condescension:

> So weeping, smiling, greet I thee, my earth,
> And do thee favours with my royal hands.
>> iii. 2. 10–11

To describe Richard as a poet would discount the importance of critical self-awareness in good writing, but in one sense the description is justified. He has the power of using words creatively, to produce impressions of reality strong enough to overpower his perception of material actuality. His misfortune is that he alone is deluded by these shadows of reality. He cannot realise that the splendid role with which he identifies himself has no more substance than an actor's part, and is not the basis of his individuality. The effortless majesty and power which he continually tries to project has no more actuality than his creative eloquence can give, and Richard does not recognise that his words make no impression upon political facts. How badly he deludes himself becomes evident when he is confronted by the direct challenge of Bolingbroke's insurrection. The danger will dissolve without exertion on Richard's part: stones will be transformed into armed warriors, the rebels will be overthrown by angelic intervention, or shamed into surrender by the mere appearance of their true sovereign:

> So when this thief, this traitor Bolingbroke . . .
> Shall see us rising in our throne, the east,
> His treasons will sit blushing in his face,
> Not able to endure the sight of day.
>> iii. 2. 47–52

This fantasy of himself as *le roi soleil* is fathered by

Richard's belief that as crowned monarch he must possess the irresistible powers which he associates with the name of king. The scene with Gaunt at Ely House suggests how far the title itself represents the personal majesty which Richard assumes his own. He appears to shrug off Gaunt's rebuke of his prodigality until it reaches the denial of his royal title:

> Landlord of England art thou now, not king.
>
> ii. 1. 113

At this his rage boils over. Gaunt has committed the unpardonable crime of disputing Richard's right to the name on which his whole identity depends, and must feel the weight of the King's uncontrolled fury. Later, when Bolingbroke's rapid exploitation of success strikes away Richard's supports one after another, the King is momentarily dislodged from his royal *persona* and has to be prompted to recall who he is. 'I had forgot myself,' he admits;

> Am I not king? . . .
> Is not the king's name twenty thousand names?
> Arm, arm, my name; a puny subject strikes
> At thy great glory.
>
> iii. 2. 83–87

Richard could not show more explicitly how far he has sunk his individual self in his royal title. He has indeed forgotten himself. Mesmerised by the bare name of king, he makes over to it all the authority which he should command by force of character, attributing to it supernatural powers of multiplying itself and of acting with irresistible energy. The full shock of political disaster compels Richard to acknowledge the emptiness of his grand identity, and to fall back towards the simply human character whose development he has ignored.

55

'You have but mistook me all this while,' he complains
to his followers, not recognising how much more seriously
he has been mistaken in himself;

> I live with bread like you, feel want,
> Taste grief, need friends; subjected thus,
> How can you say to me, I am a king?
>
> iii. 2. 175–7

The play on words betrays his levity. As Richard senses
that he is losing grasp of his kingly name, he attempts
to fit himself into another role, as pathetic as the first had
been splendid; but again without means of becoming the
part. When he fails to bluff Bolingbroke into submission,
'because we thought ourselves thy lawful king', he has no
reserves of personality to fill up the gap left by his
dwindling title. The exchange between York and Northumberland before the meeting at Flint indicates how
rapidly Richard is losing the respect due to his royal name.
Northumberland remarks that Richard is close at hand,
and is rebuked for speaking so unceremoniously:

> It would beseem the Lord Northumberland
> To say, 'King Richard': alack, the heavy day,
> When such a sacred king should hide his head!
>
> iii. 3. 7–9

Northumberland defends his neglect of protocol: 'only to
be brief Left I his title out'; but this political realist knows
that Richard's claim to be king is now more than ever a
form of words. The awesome figure of majesty and the
negligible human being who has tried to fill the role are
about to be separated. As Richard sees himself about to
be humiliated by Bolingbroke's political triumph, he
wishes he might be as great as his grief 'or lesser than
my name', unconscious that he has always fallen short of
its magnificence. The prospect of losing his title is a

threat of becoming personally nameless, and the most painful form of deprivation that he can suffer:

> What must the king do now? must he submit?
> The king shall do it. Must he be deposed?
> The king shall be contented. Must he lose
> The name of king?
>
> iii. 3. 143–6

Before his deposition he makes a pathetic effort to reassert the mystical authority of his lost name, by crying, 'God save the king!' to the assembly of nobles; making a final appeal to their loyalty and to the power which, Carlisle had assured him, would keep him king 'in spite of all'. No one answers. Richard must play clerk to his own priest, making the response to his own prayer, and acknowledge himself dispossessed:

> God save the king, although I be not he.
>
> iv. 1. 174

The formal act of deposition follows. Invited to resign the crown, Richard swings between contradictory impulses, 'Ay, no; no, ay:' and then resolves his indecision by an answer which allows him to play on the sense of the words he has just used: 'for I must nothing be'. So far from offering resistance, he himself carries out the sentence which strips him of majesty, rights and possessions, and reduces him to an anonymous cypher. He begins characteristically by calling his audience to attention—'Mark me how I will undo myself'—and then begins to cancel out his own existence by a piecemeal dismembering of himself. Richard not only gives up the name and authority of king, but spends what remains of his royal power in bankrupting the estate which he has possessed:

> With mine own tears I wash away my balm,
> With mine own hands I give away my crown,

> With mine own tongue deny my sacred state,
> With mine own breath release all duteous oaths.
>
>   iv. 1. 207–10

By the end of the ceremony and his final exercise of
kingly rights, Richard has effectively ceased to exist;
and although Northumberland is eager to press charges
against the human nonentity whom he has become,
Richard's question, 'What more remains?' invites his
audience to recognise how completely he has destroyed
himself. As Northumberland persists, he goads Richard
into an outburst of self-pitying indignation, and an
acknowledgement of the nameless being which is his new
character:

> No lord of thine, thou haught insulting man,
> Nor no man's lord: I have no name, no title;
> No, not that name was given me at the font,
> But 'tis usurped. Alack the heavy day,
> That I have worn so many winters out,
> And know not now what name to call myself!
>
>   iv. 1. 254–9

This consciousness is not tragic, for Richard finds in
being nobody a distinction which compensates for his
ignominious loss of majesty. From this point his behaviour leaves the impression of a man wilfully bent upon
destroying himself. Earlier, Gaunt has diagnosed such
an impulse in Richard by describing him as 'possessed
now to depose thyself'; a warning not much weakened
by the play on words. Richard surrenders himself to
Bolingbroke as though he wished to ensure his political
abasement, hinting broadly at Bolingbroke's larger
ambition before there has been any show of an attempt
on the crown. His deliberateness of manner at his
deposition, when he ceremoniously takes the king to

pieces, deepens the impression that Richard is set upon self-obliteration. To object that Shakespeare could not have seen Richard's behaviour in these terms does not invalidate the impression; in fact, Gaunt helps us to accept it. His warning that Richard is insanely determined to reduce himself to nothing is borne out in Richard's prayer at the end of his abjuration of rights:

> Make me, that nothing have, with nothing grieved.
> iv. i. 216

He moves towards the state of nothingness as towards the satisfaction of a perverse desire. Although he has insisted that his rights and title are inviolable, he is not prepared to undertake the simplest physical measures to defend them. If the stones will not rise against Bolingbroke, and no angelic host fight the King's battles for him, then Richard must contract out of the political system which has refused to substantiate his idea of the king. He retires into a world of private fantasy, where hard facts cannot impinge disrespectfully upon the royal performance of which he is now sole spectator.

In banishing Bolingbroke at Coventry, Richard had been impelled less by political motives than by a wish to be rid of a rival whose solid substantiality stood as a mock to his own pretensions to kingly power. Bolingbroke's popularity with the common people piques Richard, as though depriving him of adulation that he should receive by right; but he is more deeply irked by his inability to impose his royal will upon Bolingbroke's tougher spirit. When he tries to force the quarrelling nobles to make peace, his comment,

> We were not born to sue, but to command;
> i. i. 196

reminds Richard as well as his two angry subjects of the
royal authority which should prove itself in their obedience. Put to the test, this notion of kingly power collides
with the defiant will of the disputants and collapses
ignominiously: a rebuff whose humiliation Richard repays
at Coventry. By interrupting the combat he is making a
purely wilful manifestation of power, designed to reinstate
his damaged self-esteem at the expense of ordered ritual.
Instead of allowing the combat to run its course he takes
judgement into his own hands, making it the instrument
of private malice, and ridding himself of the figure whose
innate sovereignty tacitly discredits Richard's efforts to
fill the role of king. His savage treatment of Mowbray
suggests that Richard lacks the nerve to impose a drastic
sentence on the man whom he is most anxious to put
out of his kingdom. By reducing Bolingbroke's term of
banishment he hopes to induce his rival to go quietly into
exile without suspecting—as Richard hints to Aumerle—
that he will not be allowed to return.

Resentment of Bolingbroke's natural authority is the
motive of Richard's behaviour after the death of Gaunt,
when he seizes Lancaster's estates, denies Bolingbroke
access to his inheritance, and allows his favourites to
erase all marks of ancestral right from the banished man's
properties. The sober truth behind Gaunt's remark,
'Thou dost seek to kill my name in me', is now revealed.
Richard is trying to put a stop to the house of Lancaster,
whose heir discredits Richard's royal performance merely
by showing the authentic personal authority of a king.
Banishment, dispossession and outlawry are intended to
reduce Bolingbroke to a penniless nobody; the shadow of a
man deprived of name and legal rights, and permanently
excluded from the kingdom to which he seems naturally

entitled. Ironically, it is Richard who suffers the personal obliteration which he designs for Bolingbroke. The attempt to starve Bolingbroke of substance recoils upon Richard as the banished man springs back upon him in the assurance of superior power. It is not Richard whose dazzling sovereignty puts the shamefaced pretender to flight. The contest between the two claimants is quickly resolved, Richard's authority proving a sham as the pressure of Bolingbroke's substance is brought to bear. Where a political interpretation of the play sees a lawful king deposed by a sacrilegious usurper, the imaginative purposes of *Richard II* centre upon a confrontation of a majestic imposture by the robust reality it has attempted to evade. Despite its lack of legality, Bolingbroke's claim to the crown has a natural cogency which discredits Richard's title without recourse to argument. When he speaks after his deposition of having been 'outfaced by Bolingbroke', Richard acknowledges that his royal bluff has been called.

The relationship of the two men, with one another and with the crown, is embodied in a dramatic image during the deposition scene. While Richard prepares to relinquish his rights the two claimants stand, each with a hand on the crown, facing one another across the symbol of majesty. Richard cannot let the moment pass without moralising:

> Now is this golden crown like a deep well
> That owes two buckets, filling one another;
> The emptier ever dancing in the air,
> The other down, unseen, and full of water.
>
> iv. 1. 184–7

His application of the simile is typically mistaken. Bolingbroke, rapidly and joyfully mounting up, is represented by the empty bucket; while Richard, 'down, and full of tears', is its heavy and submerged counterpart. One of the royal gardeners shows a more realistic appreciation of the political weight of the two men. 'In your lord's scale,' he tells the Queen,

> is nothing but himself,
> And some few vanities that make him light;
> But in the balance of great Bolingbroke,
> Besides himself, are all the English peers,
> And with that odds he weighs King Richard down.
>
> iii. 4. 85–89

The empty bucket, 'dancing in the air', could only represent the shallow frivolity of Richard, who even at this moment of disaster hunts after literary conceits, as the weight and fullness of the other symbolise Bolingbroke's political mastery. However much Richard looks like a king, he could only fill up his empty account by stealing Bolingbroke's substance, and his intended victim has reversed the process.

The speech typifies Richard's habitual commerce with shadows and bodiless forms, the creation of a self-indulgent fancy which leads him always further from true judgement. In this respect he and the Queen speak with the same voice, using language to construct elaborate mazes of ideas or to play off the senses of words against each other, and to immobilise active thought. During the King's absence in Ireland, Bushy tries to reassure the Queen by arguing that her premonition of bad news springs from nothing substantial:

> Each substance of a grief hath twenty shadows,
> Which shows like grief itself, but is not so.
>
> ii. 2. 14–15

She is considering Richard's absence from a distorting standpoint, Bushy continues, and so finding

> shapes of grief more than himself to wail;
> Which looked on as it is, is nought but shadows
> Of what it is not.
>
> ii. 2. 22–24

In turning about the theme of substance and shadow, his argument makes a point of general importance to the play. Bushy's reference to the shadow which seems 'like grief itself, but is not so' opens a wider field of allusion in which Richard too is involved. The Queen answers Bushy by an ingenious improvisation upon the points of his argument, doubling upon the sense of words to produce a tangle of paradox and conceit which is the only justification of her speech:

> For nothing hath begot my something grief,
> Or something hath the nothing that I grieve;
> 'Tis in reversion that I do possess,
> But what it is, that is not yet known what,
> I cannot name, 'tis nameless woe, I wot.
>
> ii. 2. 36–40

The nothing which I am, the Queen appears to be saying, has fathered this real substance, grief: implying that her grief is the only real thing about her. The argument, designed to prove its speaker a bodiless fantasy, wastes verbal ingenuity upon a trifling purpose in a fashion characteristic of Richard. He too argues, when deposition has taken all his substance from him, that his griefs alone give him weight. In this he is as badly mistaken as the Queen, who in Bushy's diagnosis 'for things true, weeps things imaginary'. The sorrows which—as Richard supposes—weigh him down by their heavy bulk are the empty creations of his fancy; shadows of grief which, according to Bushy, sorrow's eye, 'glazed with blinding tears', cannot distinguish from real substance.

The extent of Richard's commitment to this world of bodiless forms is shown immediately after his deposition, when he asks for a mirror;

> That it may show me what a face I have
> Since it is bankrupt of his majesty.
>
> iv. i. 266–7

The request reveals the closed circuit of Richard's consciousness. He is willingly imprisoned within himself, absorbed by a sterile relationship with his own reflection, which flatters him with his own self-admiring gaze. On this occasion the mirror fails him. Instead of the tragic face which Richard expects, it offers him a familiar expression showing no marks of grief. Either his face has never borne the stamp of majesty, or his griefs are as shallow as the 'things imaginary' which had troubled the Queen. Exasperated by its refusal to echo his tragic mood, he smashes the glass, following a characteristic impulse to destroy whatever intrudes upon his private fantasy, and calls upon Bolingbroke to observe the moral of the incident: 'How soon my sorrow hath destroyed my face.' Bolingbroke's close preoccupation with the world of fact makes him scorn word-play, but he meets the occasion with a discerning comment:

> The shadow of your sorrow hath destroyed
> The shadow of your face.
>
> iv. i. 292–3

Richard is momentarily taken aback by the neatness of the rejoinder, but then pounces upon this new paradox and develops it further:

64

'Tis very true; my grief lies all within,
And these external manner of laments
Are merely shadows to the unseen grief
That swells with silence in the tortured soul:
There lies the substance.

iv. i. 295–9

His gloss does not represent Bolingbroke's intention.
Grief has so darkened your mind, the polite sense of his
remark runs, that you have smashed your reflection in the
glass. Under cover of this simple comment, his perceptive
understanding of Richard has offered a second observation,
knowing that it would pass unnoticed. Your reflection
in the glass, he has told Richard, is a thing as insubstantial as the grief which, you say, has made you smash
the mirror. The remark has further implications, but its
chief significance lies in its discrediting of Richard's
moral, by describing both his sorrow and his face as
shadows. What Richard takes to be substantial, Bolingbroke knows to be illusory and bodiless. Richard overlooks the more cryptic meaning of Bolingbroke's comment
in the empty interest of elaborating fresh conceits from
the original paradox, and of providing new proofs of
the reality of his grief. His demonstration is as self-
defeating as the Queen's attempt to prove herself non-
existent. The flimsiness of the argument, and the triviality
of mind which it reveals, are incompatible with the weight
of grief which Richard affects to be bearing.

As a prisoner in Pomfret Castle, Richard is cut off
from all relationship with the outside world and denied
communication with other beings. His physical circumstances as a prisoner, caged-up inside granite walls with
'not a creature but myself', represent the psychological
state to which Richard has always tended. His immature

habit of thrusting disconcerting facts out of sight, and of substituting fantasy for unpalatable truth to protect his self-esteem, has now hardened into a condition which he has no power to cast off. Because he has refused to come to terms with personal and political realities, he is now confined within the state of being which he has always preferred, beyond contact with actuality and obliged to act as audience to himself. His only society is a company of phantasmal creatures, begotten upon himself:

> My brain I'll prove the female to my soul,
> My soul the father; and these two beget
> A generation of still-breeding thoughts;
> And these same thoughts people this little world.
>
> v. 5. 6–9

This bodiless offspring, multiplying like a cloud of gnats, is the only progeny which Richard could produce. He has played with words, treating them as though they embodied reality and gave the speaker possession of their substance. Now he tries to generate forms through the sterile commerce of words alone, enacting male and female roles in his single self, much as he sought relationship with the mirror-self reflected in a glass. The paradoxes and doublings of verbal sense which have delighted Richard now turn against him as he struggles to establish some unequivocal truth. Thoughts of things divine, he discovers,

> are intermixed
> With scruples, and do set the word itself
> Against the word.
>
> v. 5. 12–14

His soliloquy becomes an attempt to hammer out some analogy between the world at large and Richard's cell, where the eddies of his unstable purpose will duplicate the wide range of human temperament in society. In fact, his comparisons illuminate only Richard's capacity for assuming character-parts, none of them realised in any depth, and leave no impression of a more substantial identity beneath. Eventually he abandons the performance, admitting its shallowness:

> Thus play I in one person many people,
> And none contented.
>
> v. 5. 31f.

The instability of character which he has always shown dominates him as he swings in thought between extremes of personal circumstance, passing from sovereignty to beggary and back again as conflicting impulses pluck at him, and ending in nothing:

> Sometimes am I king;
> Then treason makes me wish myself a beggar,
> And so I am. Then crushing penury
> Persuades me I was better when a king:
> Then am I kinged again; and by and by
> Think that I am unkinged by Bolingbroke,
> And straight am nothing.
>
> v. 5. 32–38

His mind works without real purpose, best pleased when it can admire the effect of what he enacts in the mixed role of king and nobody. In his last scene Richard describes himself perceptively as an actor who runs perfunctorily through a variety of parts without discovering any character in which he can sink himself. He can bring nothing substantial to the part he plays. When he is robbed of his leading role as king, he turns towards nothingness as the only state which promises him satisfaction:

67

Whate'er I be,
Nor I, nor any man that but man is,
With nothing shall be pleased, till he be eased
With being nothing.

v. 5. 38–41

The seriousness of the remark is sacrificed for the trivial
pleasure of word-play, and the part is denied importance.
In his taste for frivolity Richard has always been pleased
with nothing, and it is poetically just that he should
become a completely anonymous being. As the central
character of the deposition scene he tries to present himself as a tragic figure; but although deeply moved by his
own performance he can give the part no weight, and his
audience remains stonily unmoved. As later his attempt
to populate his cell with 'still-breeding thoughts' suggests his inability to invest his ideas with vital substance,
so generally Richard's acting proves the insubstantiality
of the private self behind the being who tries to exist in
the role he plays.

The character which Richard has tried to invest with
body is exposed to a public test on the day of Bolingbroke's
coronation, and is laughed off the stage as a sham. York,
who describes the scene, feels pity for Richard; but he
admits how much more convincingly Bolingbroke fills
the part which Richard had tried to make his own. The
theatrical analogy, with its reference to the bad actor's
tedious prattle, provides a thoroughly damaging comment
on the whole of Richard's performance in the role now
taken over by Bolingbroke:

As, in a theatre, the eyes of men
After a well-graced actor leaves the stage,
Are idly bent on him that enters next,

Thinking his prattle to be tedious,
Even so—or with much more contempt—men's eyes
Did scowl on Richard.

v. 2. 23–28

Invited to make a direct comparison between two interpretations of the same part, the crowd howls derision at
Richard's performance and pelts him with rubbish.
Bolingbroke, meanwhile, is given the tumultuous welcome
of a popular idol, and acknowledges the applause with the
deference of a man born to easy mastery; 'bare-headed,
lower than his proud steed's neck'. His arrival brings the
city to life. 'You would have thought the very windows
spake,' York comments,

> and that all the walls
> With painted imagery had said at once,
> 'Jesu preserve thee, welcome, Bolingbroke!'

v. 2. 15–17

The idea of inanimate things bursting into life is not
easily reconciled with the simple conception of Bolingbroke as usurper. The roar of acclamation from the city
suggests a great upsurge of vitality which Richard had
been unable to transmit. By deposing this lay figure of
kingship and taking over his crucial office, Bolingbroke
reinvigorates the kingdom, as though releasing it from a
spell. Richard has himself admitted his sterility by dis-
charging his remaining followers at Flint Castle,

> Let them go
> To ear the land that hath some hope to grow,
> For I have none.

iii. 2. 211–13

The self-pitying tone of the speech proves the point he is
making. Like other Shakespearean characters who

69

become absorbed in the pathos of their own situation, Richard has no creative energy to spend on the world about him, for his narcissism starves him of substance. He recognises only at the end of his life that self-admiration has drained him of vitality to no purpose: 'I wasted time, and now doth time waste me.' Yet even here Richard cannot break himself of the trivial habit of playing with words, and the hard truth of his comment is turned aside into frivolity.

If Richard ever becomes critically aware of his weakness, his discovery never acquires tragic force. He diagnoses his personal condition accidentally, in the course of developing a pathetic conceit as he faces the humiliation of losing his crown:

> O that I were a mockery king of snow
> Standing before the sun of Bolingbroke,
> To melt myself away in water-drops!
> iv. i. 260–2

The image appeals to Richard by suggesting a tearful dissolution, where tears are unfailingly moving, but his conceit acknowledges the want of substance which exposure to Bolingbroke has found out. As sovereign he is, in effect, melting away as he speaks before the vital energy of the authentic king-figure whose splendour he had claimed for himself. His wish to be a mockery king, dissolving at the touch of Bolingbroke's solid reality, is expressed as a momentary whim; but it describes the actual relationship of the two men more accurately than Richard is able to realise.

Bolingbroke has shown his force of character much earlier. When he is banished, his father tries to palliate the distress of exile by offering fanciful consolations.

'Suppose devouring pestilence hangs in our air,' Gaunt suggests; and he advises Bolingbroke to imagine himself moving towards, and not away from whatever he most loves:

> Suppose the singing birds musicians,
> The grass whereon thou tread'st the presence strew'd,
> The flowers fair ladies, and thy steps no more
> Than a delightful measure or a dance.
>
> i. 3. 288–91

Such make-believe consolation protects Richard against unwelcome facts, but Bolingbroke has no inclination to delude himself by charming fantasy. However painful, the sensations of reality form a currency which he refuses to debase. 'Who can hold a fire in his hand,' he objects,

> By thinking on the frosty Caucasus?
> Or cloy the hungry edge of appetite
> By bare imagination of a feast?
>
> i. 3. 295–7

His speech gives further proof of the unsentimental outlook which Bolingbroke has already shown by making no protest against the sentence of banishment. His reticence puzzles Gaunt, but Richard's extravagant lamentations later in the play point the significance of Bolingbroke's sparing use of words. When he returns from exile he is too scornful of bare thanks, 'the exchequer of the poor', to offer his supporters more than a brief show of gratitude; and he is never in danger of confusing the categories of speech and action. His restraint in misfortune and his rejection of imaginary comfort prove before the end of Act I how wide a disparity of outlook separates him from Richard. He has no faith in the magic power of words to achieve political ends, and no disposition to waste himself upon fantasies of personal magnificence. During the deposition scene this economy of speech irritates Richard, as though he realised that Bolingbroke's silence was a sign of mastery, and of contempt for Richard's squandering of potential upon a charade. When Bolingbroke has been publicly acclaimed king, and Richard is walled up inside Pomfret Castle with his aimless ruminations, both men have reached a natural culmination of growth. Bolingbroke has taken control of the political organism through which he will extend his domination of material events. Richard, ruined by his addiction to fantasy, is now irrevocably lost in the mirror-world of his own mind, unable to exert any influence on the current of political affairs or to answer the challenge of external reality which it represents.

Two such challenges confront Bolingbroke as soon as he begins to rule, each the counterpart of a threat which Richard had been unable to dominate. Bagot's accusation of Aumerle, supported and denied by an increasing number of witnesses, places Bolingbroke in the same predicament as Richard had faced when Mowbray was indicted. Both accusations are violent and contradictory, as before, and the task of arbitrating between so many conflicting statements is appreciably more difficult. Bolingbroke takes firm hold of the situation. His order, 'Bring forth Bagot', has a businesslike brevity altogether lacking in the flowery elegance of Richard's address. Where Richard tries to patch a deadly quarrel with a trivial joke, Bolingbroke does not intervene in the conflict; and he concludes the hearing with a cold assertion of authority:

> Lords, you that here are under our arrest,
> Procure your sureties for your days of answer.
>
> iv. i. 158–9

A more serious challenge comes from the Abbot of

Westminster's plot to assassinate Bolingbroke and reinstate the deposed king. This conspiracy is much more dangerous than Bolingbroke's exploitation of Richard's weakness. The new king is opposed by an organised faction who can claim it their moral duty to conspire against the usurper, who has no legal title to the crown. But where Richard surrendered to an unspoken ultimatum, Bolingbroke moves instantly to defend his questionable authority. The fact that his own brother-in-law is among the conspirators does not weaken his determination to crush the plot at once and without mercy. York is dispatched

> to order several powers
> To Oxford, or where'er these traitors are:
> They shall not live within this world, I swear,
> But I will have them if I once know where.
>
> v. 3. 138–41

Richard had felt a more sentimental concern for the blood-relationship between himself and the man who deposed him.

To this actual blood-tie Richard adds a fanciful relationship, that of father to his youthful inheritor. The prospect of deposition offers him the agreeable paradox of handing down his possessions to an heir the same age as himself.[1] The conceit contains a dangerous hint that Richard will not resist Bolingbroke's growing ambition, but the attraction of the idea is too much for Richard's sense of discretion, even when he has just surrendered to his enemy:

> Cousin, I am too young to be your father,
> Though you are old enough to be my heir.
> What you will have, I'll give, and willing too.
>
> iii. 3. 204–6

[1] Both men were thirty-two at the time.

The point recurs in York's report that Richard has agreed to abdicate, and to adopt Bolingbroke as his heir. These hints of a father–son relationship between the two cousins contribute to the working-out of a theme which involves most of the chief characters of *Richard II*. Many of the references to family relationship are put in a form which allows sons and fathers to be mentioned, although the kinship is less direct. Gaunt addresses his nephew Richard as 'my brother Edward's son', and then describes himself as 'his father Edward's son', making his point at the expense of clarity. When Richard sets aside his relationship with the appellant Bolingbroke, he confuses their actual kinship in a similar way, choosing to be roundabout for the sake of referring to another family tie:

> Were he my brother, nay, my kingdom's heir,
> As he is but my father's brother's son.
>
> i. 1. 116f.

Instead of describing the relationships between descendants of Edward III directly, Shakespeare makes the speaker trace the son's line of descent back to the father, and to the ancestor whom he shares with the second character. York does not describe himself simply as uncle to Richard, but as

> the last of noble Edward's sons,
> Of whom thy father, Prince of Wales, was first.
>
> ii. 1. 171f.

When Bolingbroke returns from exile, now fatherless, he is met by a Lord Regent who rejects his first appeal to kinship—'uncle me no uncle'—but who then yields to the suggestion that Bolingbroke should be considered as an adopted son. 'You are my father,' Bolingbroke tells him, 'for methinks in you I see old Gaunt alive.' Reminding

York that he too has a son, 'Aumerle, my noble cousin', Bolingbroke argues that had this son been so abused after the death of York,

> He should have found his uncle Gaunt a father.
>
> ii. 3. 126

The remark has ambiguous overtones. Behind its immediate suggestion of close family loyalty, Bolingbroke seems to imply that Gaunt's status was as equivocal as the relationship he claims for himself when he assumes the identity of York's son. Bolingbroke might be figuratively dispossessing Aumerle, as he will dispossess his royal cousin in fact. As though responding to his presumption, Aumerle will join the faction seeking to unseat Bolingbroke, to be bought off by his mother's appeal to the King against York's insistence that he shall be punished as a traitor.

The father-son relationships of *Richard II* are developed in part as a form of conceit with no more imaginative consequence than the verbal quibbles which characterise the play. But in the parallels which they set up between different pairs of characters, they constitute a mode of ironic commentary by which Shakespeare reveals moral contradictions not recognised by the speakers themselves. The fact that York, like Bolingbroke, is the father of a troublesome son invites this form of unspoken commentary by parallel. When his son's part in the conspiracy is disclosed, York is thrown into a frenzy of anxiety to prove his own loyalty, and insists that Aumerle should not be pardoned. His behaviour contrasts sharply with Gaunt's attitude towards the banishing of his son:

> You urged me as a judge, but I had rather
> You would have bid me argue like a father . . .

75

A partial slander[1] sought I to avoid,
And in the sentence my own life destroyed.

i. 3. 237–42

York's argument against clemency involves a denial of
the natural bond between father and son. It also exactly
reverses Gaunt's position by asserting that the course of
strict justice that destroys the son will regenerate the
father:

> Mine honour lives when his dishonour dies,
> Or my shamed life in his dishonour lies:
> Thou kill'st me in his life; giving him breath
> The traitor lives, the true man's put to death.

v. 3. 68–71

Both situation and argument are deeply ironic. York is
pleading for strict justice from a king without legal right
to his judicial authority. He is also demanding that the
man who adopted him as father shall pass sentence of
death upon his proper son, Aumerle. These ironies are
compounded in the personal dishonour which York has
brought upon himself by surrendering Richard's power
to Bolingbroke. As regent, he has acted as treacherously
to his king as Aumerle to the usurper, and deserves the
punishment he is demanding for his son. 'Thou kill'st me
in his life' is meant to signify that the living traitor
Aumerle will be a perpetual reproach to his father; but
the remark also means that Aumerle's continuing loyalty
to the true king puts the traitor York to shame. The
father's anxiety to see the son executed takes its stronger
motive from the unacknowledged disgrace of a betrayal
far more dishonourable than Aumerle's.

The ironies of the scene go further. Bolingbroke turns
in horror from the 'heinous, strong and bold conspiracy'

[1] The reputation of a judge swayed by private interest.

which York has uncovered, to praise the integrity of the
father who has just betrayed his own child:

> O loyal father of a treacherous son!
> Thou sheer, immaculate and silver fountain
> From whence this stream, through muddy passages
> Hath held his current, and defiled himself!
> Thy overflow of good converts to bad.
>
> v. 3. 58–62

In fact Aumerle has followed the example of his father's
disloyalty to the reigning king. Addressed to York,
Bolingbroke's remarks are badly misapplied, and become
fully—and ironically—appropriate only when they are
associated with Bolingbroke's own father, whom its terms
immediately suggest. Quite unconsciously, Bolingbroke is
supplying a double moral commentary upon himself, by
admiring the integrity of a confederate who shares his
own dishonour, and by lamenting the disgrace which a
dissolute son has brought upon the noble reputation of
his father; by implication, upon Gaunt. The complex
ironies of the scene are finally wound up by the disclosure that Bolingbroke is himself the father of a riotous
son. Hal has not been mentioned hitherto. The opening
phase of the scene introduces him through Bolingbroke's
worried enquiry,

> Can no man tell me of my unthrifty son?
>
> v. 3. 1

Allusions to Hal's life among the London stews and
taverns with 'unrestrained loose companions' build up
the picture of an unruly wastrel. The sudden appearance
of Aumerle interrupts the discussion without shifting the
subject very far; one dishonourable son replacing another,
and York taking over Bolingbroke's character of virtuous

father outraged by the moral degeneracy of his heir. Bolingbroke overlooks the parallel between himself and York, and neither parent recognises that his son's ignoble behaviour acts as mirror to the father's unacknowledged guilt.

The accumulated ironies of this scene show that Shakespeare is now imaginatively involved in the moral aspects of Bolingbroke's actions. The contest between Bolingbroke and Richard interests him mainly as a struggle between the substance and the shadow of kingship, in which the moral implications of usurped rule are very lightly treated. In the latter part of *Richard II* Shakespeare becomes concerned with the contradictions of Bolingbroke's position as usurper. No moral judgement is offered. Carlisle's warning of the disasters which must follow usurpation—

> The blood of English shall manure the ground,
> And future ages groan for this foul act
>
> iv. i. 137–8

—seems a true prophesy, but is too simple an explanation of the disorder and violence represented in *Henry VI* to be mistaken for an editorial comment. Like Richard's claim to be 'the deputy elected by the Lord' whom no mortal power can depose, Carlisle's warning characterises the speaker without illuminating Shakespeare's private opinion. We can feel more certain of Shakespeare's editorial presence where the ironies of a speech reveal a dangerous want of self-awareness in the speaker. By using irony in this way, Shakespeare provides an oblique commentary on moral character without appearing to intervene. Such commentary upon York and Bolingbroke is made through the unrecognised sense of their discussion over Aumerle. Although their valuation of personal honour and family reputation exposes the instinctive duplicity of both men, it leaves these standards intact as a basis of moral judgement by which all three speakers are condemned. For the ironies to be effective, the standards must be consciously implanted in the play by its author. His characters are to be judged only by the moral standards which the play itself proposes.

By this oblique means Bolingbroke is made to provide a moral commentary upon himself, not in the general terms which Carlisle might use but within a particular context of ideas which are developed steadily from the earliest scenes of *Richard II*. The remark, 'O loyal father of a treacherous son!' with its covert application to Bolingbroke and to Gaunt, reaches back further and spreads into the body of the play from a more distant historical source. Gaunt, York, and Bolingbroke are overshadowed by the legendary figure of the great warrior-king to whom they are all related. For Richard, the reputation of a famous grandfather is joined with the nobility and heroism of his father, the Black Prince; but he fails ignominiously to match his great ancestors. Gaunt does not spare Richard when he describes his debasing of a noble reputation:

> O had thy grandsire, with a prophet's eye,
> Seen how his son's son should destroy his sons,
> From forth thy reach he would have laid thy shame,
> Deposing thee before thou wert possessed.
>
> ii. 1. 104–7

Apart from its criticism of a son who dishonours his ancestry, the speech includes a reference to the killing of fathers by sons which is developed as a theme of the play. Gaunt's rebuke is seconded by York later in the same scene, when Richard resolves to seize Lancaster's estates to redeem his own bankruptcy. Speaking of the Black Prince, York protests:

> His noble hand
> Did win what he did spend, and spent not that
> Which his triumphant father's hand had won.
>
> ii. 1. 179–81

The contrast between thrift and prodigality provides a moral positive by which other characters than Richard are judged. As king, Richard has ignored his illustrious father's example, emptying his treasury and squandering his noble heritage to the point where crippling taxes and enforced levies cannot restore his credit. This is the disgrace, Gaunt argues, which Edward III might have avoided by denying Richard's right of succession after the death of his father. When York discovers Aumerle's part in the conspiracy against Bolingbroke he shows a similar eagerness to obstruct his son's inheritance, using the same images of prodigality and wastefulness to enforce his argument. Insisting that Aumerle must not be pardoned, he tells Bolingbroke:

> So shall my virtue be his vice's bawd,
> And he shall spend mine honour with his shame,
> As thriftless sons their scraping father's gold.
>
> v. 3. 65–67

But York himself has squandered a noble patrimony by betraying Richard, and the character of a prodigal son who has wasted a rich inheritance fits him better than Aumerle. The usurper who has flung away another golden estate, the time-honoured name of Lancaster, is another prodigal. The course of honourable behaviour has been marked out by Gaunt in an early scene, when he

refuses to contemplate rebellion in revenge for his
brother's death, supposedly killed at Richard's orders.
At Coventry Bolingbroke speaks respectfully of his
father's noble reputation, referring to the 'earthly author
of my blood',

> Whose youthful spirit in me regenerate,
> Doth with a twofold vigour lift me up
> To reach at victory above my head.
>
> i. 3. 70–72

Gaunt's youthful spirit may be renewed in his vigorous
son, but 'regenerate' carries moral associations which
Bolingbroke cannot apply to himself. The aspiration
which drives him reaches towards a prize, 'above my head',
nobler than he admits here, and will sever him as completely as Richard from the stem of his honourable ancestry.

The human field of *Richard II* includes four fathers, all
noble in rank if not in behaviour: Edward the Black
Prince, Gaunt, York, and Bolingbroke. Each has a son—
Richard, Bolingbroke, Aumerle, Hal—who disappoints
expectation by proving morally degenerate; a prodigal
who dissipates his inherited wealth and good name by an
ignoble course of life. Hal is not yet the enigmatic figure
of *Henry IV*, pursuing a hidden purpose under cover of
dissolute character, but the 'unthrifty son' who has been
lost among taverns and brothels for three months. In
York's judgement at least, Aumerle is another prodigal
son. Each of the four stands indicted by York's commen-
dation of the noblest of sons, Edward the Black Prince,
who 'spent not that which his triumphant father's hand
had won', whether knightly honour or revenue. The
theme of the prodigal who wastes his patrimony, dishonours a respected name, and burdens his father with
disgrace, is repeated in these central characters of *Richard*

II, and in the relationships they assume with one another. Gaunt admonishes Richard's wastefulness in the figure of a father, the traitor Bolingbroke asks to be recognised as adopted son to York, and Richard gives the idea some further currency by acknowledging himself too young to be Bolingbroke's father. The royal gardeners reinforce the theme in speaking of the apricots

> Which, like unruly children, make their sire
> Stoop with oppression of their prodigal weight.
>
> iii. 4. 30f.

This persistent knot of ideas, firmly attached to the historical framework of *Richard II*, is quickened by new interest when Shakespeare returns to the adjoining field of events in *Henry IV*. Falstaff describes his wretched conscripts as so many tattered prodigals, lately come from swine-keeping, and proposes 'the story of the Prodigal . . . in waterwork' as decoration for Quickly's dining-chamber. The figure of the royal prodigal dominates much of the play, and the father–son theme developed in *Richard II* is revived with fresh imaginative vitality. Hal's supposed theft of the crown—an act of obvious moral significance in Bolingbroke's heir—allows Shakespeare to renew and elaborate familiar concepts with a rush of creative excitement. Bolingbroke begins his soliloquy with an *exclamatio* whose ironies pass over him, 'How quickly nature falls into revolt When gold becomes her object!' and then takes the prodigal as general theme in a speech of sharply realised images:

> For this the foolish over-careful fathers
> Have broke their sleep with thoughts,
> Their brains with care, their bones with industry;
> For this they have engrossed and piled up
> The cankered heaps of strange-achieved gold . . .

When, like the bee, culling from every flower
The virtuous sweets,
Our thighs packed with wax, our mouths with honey,
We bring it to the hive; and like the bees,
Are murdered for our pains. This bitter taste
Yields his engrossments to the ending father.

Pt. 2, iv. 5. 67–79

The speech is in part an ironic reflection of the outcome of the political ambition which drove Bolingbroke to snatch the crown. His struggle to retain the 'strange-achieved gold' of kingship in defiance of moral right has broken him; and the crown seems to have aroused a similar murderous greed in the son who should inherit his achievement. The figure of the impatient son, seizing honour 'with boist'rous hand', recalls young Bolingbroke, but the King does not recognise the family likeness. The prodigal no longer represents a sudden deviation from the noble standards of his ancestry, but succeeds an avaricious father who mistook personal wealth for honour. York's reference to the riotous son who squanders a 'scraping father's gold' confirms the association of the prodigal with the miser whose wealth is without generosity. Where the Black Prince 'did win what he did spend', both Bolingbroke and York acquire their honours by committing or abetting theft, and speak of themselves appropriately as avaricious hoarders of gold. The winnings piled up by Bolingbroke—'cankered' because never put to use—have become a cumbrous load, and an encouragement to his spendthrift son to make a quick end of him.

In fact Hal merely acts the part of prodigal, and takes the crown realising what heavy obligations he must assume with it. His rightful inheritance of the crown breaks the series begun by the wastrel son of the Black

Prince and extended through other characters of *Richard
II*. Unlike Gaunt, Bolingbroke is not succeeded by a son
who steals a royal inheritance and defames a noble
reputation, but by a seeming prodigal and thief who
reverses expectation by restoring the institutions of right
and justice which both Richard and Bolingbroke had
affronted. By adopting the Lord Chief Justice as father
to his youth—an adoption which reverses the intentions
of the relationship which Bolingbroke assumes with
York—Hal brings *Henry IV* to its close on a note of
stabilised security. *Richard II* ends with no such assurance.
Bolingbroke has strengthened his grasp on the crown by
crushing Westminster's plot, but the conspiracy warns
him how uneasily he must expect to sit on Richard's
throne. Similar challenges will follow. Across his domestic
life falls the shadow of a disreputable son in whose wild
behaviour Bolingbroke tries hopefully to find promise of
future distinction. The closing scene of the play brings
news of political triumph, and of the death which elimin-
ates the major threat to Bolingbroke's doubtful authority;
but success brings an uneasy lull rather than peace. The
new king has already begun to taste the disillusion of his
stolen honour, which the end of his reign will have
darkened his whole outlook. Almost the last ironic stab
of discomfort comes from the discovery that Hal is as
impatient to possess the crown as Bolingbroke himself had
been, and that he must rebuke his own crime in his son:

> Dost thou so hunger for mine empty chair
> That thou wilt needs invest thee with mine honours
> Before thy hour be ripe?

Ibid., 94–96

Impatience for this supreme honour has been responsible
for the wasting of ancestral reputation, and for the

murder of the adoptive father who had accepted Bolingbroke as heir. In Bolingbroke the ideas which link
together fathers and sons are realised in dramatic terms,
deepening the admission of guilt which ends the play.
The actual crimes committed by Bolingbroke merge
with others suggested by associated imagery, or by
figures parallel to himself. His dismissal of Exton as a
man accursed—'With Cain go wander thorough shades
of night'—does not also drive Bolingbroke's guilt out of
doors, but suggests the moral atmosphere in which the
King must henceforward move. His hope of expiating the
crime is raised half-heartedly, as an unconvincing gesture
of remorse; and the appearance of Richard's coffin
symbolises the disquiet which will continue to oppress
Bolingbroke's reign.

In a reading of the second tetralogy centred upon
Carlisle's warning of what must follow deposition, this
guilty insecurity will appear as an aspect of the curse which
Bolingbroke brings upon himself and his kingdom by
this crime. The recurrent imaginative figures of *Richard II*
do not support this view. They trace out a pattern of
events in which a noble father is disgraced by a morally
degenerate son who flings away the fortune earned by his
great ancestors. In deposing Richard, himself such a
prodigal son, seizing his title and finally allowing his
kinsman to be murdered, Bolingbroke outrages the tradition of loyalty and probity invested in his family name
and brings lasting infamy upon himself. Once established
as king, he finds himself occupying the position of noble
father, troubled by a son in whom his own wild prodigality is renewed. The ancestral circle has come about,
and its ironic design waits to be traced out afresh from
this starting-point in the two parts of *Henry IV*.

CHAPTER III

The Royal Counterfeit

I. THE KING

THE first part of *Henry IV* followed *Richard II* after an
interval of two years, and if Chambers is right after
three intervening plays. Shakespeare's development as a
creative writer was now rapidly approaching a climax,
and although this second instalment of the tetralogy
begins more or less where *Richard II* leaves off, the two
plays do not fit together at all snugly. Seen from a
general historical point of view *Henry IV* may be regarded
as a sequel, but as an imaginative work it is independent of
Richard II, drawing its impulse from concepts which owe
little to the earlier play. The shift of outlook is immediately
clear in the changed character of Prince Hal, but Shakespeare's reappraisal of historical figures is most obvious
in the new perspective which he gives to Bolingbroke.
In *Richard II* most of the damaging criticisms levelled
at Bolingbroke by the chroniclers are intercepted,
presumably because they would have attracted more
sympathy for Richard than suited Shakespeare's
purposes. The usurper of *Henry IV* conforms more
closely with the shifty, hypocritical figure whom
Holinshed describes making his way by fraudulence and
deceit.

A simple example will show how Shakespeare turned
back to the evidence of Bolingbroke's bad faith which had
been passed over silently in *Richard II*. Holinshed
describes how, at Shrewsbury, the rebels presented to the

86

King sealed articles which 'in effect charged him with manifest perjurie',

> in that (contrarie to his oth receiued vpon the euangelists at Doncaster, when he first entred the realme after his exile) he had taken vpon him the crowne and roiall dignitie, imprisoned king Richard, caused him to resigne his title, and finallie to be murthered.[1]

This important incident, with its disclosure of a sworn assurance broken by Bolingbroke, is not mentioned in the scenes dealing with his return from exile, or brought against him by the rebels of *Richard II*. In Shakespeare's account of the usurpation there is no need for Bolingbroke to use deceit: the crown falls into his hands almost without effort on his part. But in *Henry IV* the deliberate fraudulence and bad faith which Holinshed mentions several times becomes a prominent part of Bolingbroke's character, and this incident is specifically recalled. 'You swore to us,' Worcester reminds the King before their battle,

> And you did swear that oath at Doncaster,
> That you did nothing purpose 'gainst the state.
> Pt. i, v. i. 42f.

Unlike his earlier counterpart, the Bolingbroke of *Henry IV* is a cynically adept politician who has dispossessed the rightful king by guile, having assured himself of popular support by ingratiating behaviour towards the common people, and by deflecting their loyalty from Richard to himself. Holinshed notes his popularity, remarking that when Bolingbroke was on his way to exile 'wonder it was to see what number of people ran after him in every town and street . . . lamenting and bewailing'. The other

[1] Humphreys, p. 174

chroniclers concur on this point, but neither they nor
any character in *Richard II* suggests that Bolingbroke was
welcomed to Coventry as a more popular figure than the
King. Although there are references in *Richard II* to
his 'humble and familiar courtesy' to poor artisans, and
although Richard resents this courting of popular favour,
Shakespeare does not press the point. It comes as a
surprise in *Henry IV* to hear Westmoreland recall how
completely Bolingbroke had transferred the people's
affection to himself at the time of his banishment:

> All their prayers and love
> Were set on Hereford, whom they doted on,
> And blessed and graced indeed more than the king.
>
> Pt. 2, iv. 1. 137–9

This might be seen as a partisan opinion, but Bolingbroke
admits to Hal that he had deliberately set himself to
undermine Richard's standing with his subjects by
presenting a more attractive figure:

> And then I stole all courtesy from heaven,
> And dressed myself in such humility
> That I did pluck allegiance from men's hearts . . .
> Even in the presence of the crowned king.
>
> Pt. 1, iii. 2. 50–54

There is no open hint of this purpose in *Richard II*, where
Bolingbroke attracts loyalty without effort or competition
against the king's flimsy claim to respect. His former
supporters, who are now in arms against Bolingbroke's
repudiation of his debt, cannot forgive the hypocritical
charm which won them to his cause. Hotspur, summing
him up scornfully as 'this king of smiles', describes
angrily how he had been gulled by Bolingbroke's compli-
ments at their first meeting:

> Why, what a candy deal of courtesy
> This fawning greyhound then did proffer me!
>
> Pt. 1, i. 3. 247f.

Again *Richard II* does not bear out the remark. Hotspur's first words are a spontaneous offer of service, answered in six lines of well-mannered thanks, after which their conversation turns to practical issues. A second charge, that Bolingbroke's supporters were won over by his show of concern for the misgovernment of the kingdom and his 'seeming brow of justice', bears no correspondence with the events of *Richard II*. There Bolingbroke returns professing interest only in the improper restraint of his inheritance; and Richard falls in consequence of the self-indulgent despotism which has weakened him, not through Bolingbroke's duplicity. The nobles are already disturbed by the injustice and frivolity of Richard's government, and their disquiet makes them allies without persuasion.

It is of course clear that Bolingbroke has the natural gifts of a politician and no inclination to suppress private interest when the crown appears within his grasp; but the interpretation put upon his past behaviour in *Henry IV* goes well beyond the limits of fair inference. Too much of the later Bolingbroke is incompatible with his namesake in *Richard II* for the two figures to be accepted as the same man. Like all Shakespeare's plays, *Henry IV* determines its own conditions without referring to other works with which it is nominally connected.

The shift of ground which comparison with *Richard II* reveals provides a helpful indication of Shakespeare's more complex purpose in *Henry IV*. The King is a practised hypocrite and dissembler, an oath-breaker and a confirmed bad debtor who answers his creditors with a knife. The Percies' rebellion is the direct consequence of Bolingbroke's anxiety to avoid repaying the debt he has contracted by accepting the help which allowed him to depose Richard. 'My father and my uncle and myself,' Hotspur tells Blunt indignantly,

> Did give him that same royalty he wears,
> And when he was not six and twenty strong,
> Sick in the world's regard, wretched and low,
> A poor unminded outlaw sneaking home,
> My father gave him welcome to the shore.
>
> Pt. 1, iv. 3. 55–59

Blunt shows no interest in the recital, but Bolingbroke is sharply conscious of his unacknowledged obligation to the rebels, and reacts instantly to Worcester's blunt reminder of his unpaid account. For his pointed allusion to the greatness 'which our own hands Have holp to make so portly', Worcester is dismissed from the royal presence almost before he has finished speaking; and Bolingbroke shows the same angry impatience to deny that Mortimer had rendered any service for which he should be ransomed. From the outset he appears nervously watchful for any threat to his still unstable authority, and vindictively inclined towards the fellow-conspirators with whom he is refusing to share the spoils of their joint enterprise. When Worcester argues that he and his confederates have been forced to take up arms in their own defence, he attracts a sarcastic gibe from Falstaff; but in fact he is telling the sober truth. Hotspur has already warned his associates that Bolingbroke 'studies day and night'

> To answer all the debt he owes to you,
> Even with the bloody payment of your deaths:
>
> Pt. 1, i. 3. 183f.

a judgement which Bolingbroke himself confirms later

in the play, when he confesses what steps he took to
secure himself against his disaffected friends,

> By whose fell working I was first advanced,
> And by whose power I well might lodge a fear
> To be again displaced: which to avoid
> I cut them off.
>
> Pt. 2, iv. 5. 206–9

This is less than completely honest, though damning
enough in its admission of misusing royal power to
silence private fears. Bolingbroke does not mention the
uncomfortably large debt which was cancelled when
Worcester and the Percies were eliminated. Worcester,
the most sourly disgruntled of his creditors, speaks
plainly about the royal appetite which, not content with
seizing all the booty his supporters had helped him win,
threatened to engulf them too. 'Being fed by us,' he
reminds Bolingbroke,

> you used us so
> As that ungentle gull the cuckoo's bird
> Useth the sparrow—did oppress our nest,
> Grew by our feeding to so great a bulk
> That even our love durst not come near your sight
> For fear of swallowing.
>
> Pt. 1, v. 1. 59–64

The rebellion is not prompted by self-protection alone.
Disappointed greed in Worcester, and in Hotspur a
furious determination to be quits with the man who has
cheated and outwitted them, give their plot a wild impulse
which discounts the hazards of war and brings the
rebellion to a disastrous end. Politically the rebels are no
more disinterested than Bolingbroke; but whatever un-
confessed motives impel them, they have a genuine—if
legally invalid—ground of complaint in the use which he

has made of them; carrying off the crown with their help, and then using his newly-won power to frustrate their attempts to force a settlement.

Shakespeare could have found the basis of Bolingbroke's changed character in Holinshed, who speaks of many who

> enuied the prosperous state of king Henrie, sith it was euident inough to the world, that he had with wrong vsurped the crowne, and not onlie violentlie deposed king Richard, but also cruellie procured his death.[1]

The memory of his crime is kept alive by the rebels, who regard Richard as the martyr of their political cause. The Archbishop excites popular support for the second rebellion by preaching against the sacrilegious act committed by a usurping king, and blood 'scraped from Pomfret stones' provides ghastly evidence of his unpunished crime. Northumberland, who had stage-managed the deposition for Bolingbroke, now admits his share in the guilt of Richard's death and utters a parenthetic prayer for pardon. Hotspur sees a further source of grievance in the dishonour which Bolingbroke's supporters have brought upon themselves by assisting the usurper, for whose sake they must now

> wear the detested blot
> Of murderous subornation.
> Pt. 1, i. 3. 160f.

Their spiritual remorse, and their readiness to champion Richard's lawful heir against Bolingbroke as though making amends for their wrong, are overshadowed by the rankling indignity of being 'fooled, discarded and shook

[1] Humphreys, p. 173

off', which is a major motive of their rebellion; but they are ready to speak frankly about their part in deposing Richard where Bolingbroke averts his mind from the subject. He has mainly succeeded in shutting his mind to a discreditable past, and when Hotspur describes him as 'this forgetful man' he makes one more point than he realises. There is more unrecognised meaning in the Archbishop's argument, at the climax of the second rebellion, that the King is anxious to 'wipe his tables clean',

> And keep no tell-tale to his memory
> That may repeat and history his loss
> To new remembrance.
> Pt. 2, iv. i. 202–4

His personal debts and his spiritual guilt are irksome facts which Bolingbroke evades as far as he can, adopting a façade of moral respectability which hardens into a character he himself accepts as authentic. The regal manner which he assumes does not suggest the impudence of a usurper, conscious that he is merely impersonating the king, but a monarch whose legal right is established beyond dispute. His imperviousness to the fact of being himself a successful rebel makes his high-toned dealing with the Percy faction particularly ironic, and invites the kind of satirical comment which Holinshed attributes to Hotspur after the King's 'fraudulent excuse' for not ransoming Mortimer:

> Behold, the heire of the relme is robbed of his right, and yet the robber with his owne will not redeeme him.[1]

Henry IV does not lack characters who keep the plain facts of Bolingbroke's greed, fraudulence and double-

1 Humphreys, p. 170

dealing in clear view, against the figure of unruffled majesty which he tries to present to the world.

There is some apparent disagreement over the means by which Bolingbroke acquired the crown. It is clear to the rebels that the deposition had been methodically planned, that Bolingbroke's undertakings at his return from exile were cynically insincere, and that he had never had any intention of honouring the debts he contracted to them. He remains, especially in the early scenes of the play, deeply tainted by perjury and dissimulation as well as by the unabsolved crime of Richard's death. Yet despite his long record of deceit, Bolingbroke appears genuinely unaware of the course of deliberate subversion and treachery which brought him to the throne. He speaks of his accession as though the crown had come into his hands by accident, and with no connivance on his part. When he recalls Richard's prophecy of Northumberland's fall from favour, Bolingbroke denies having had any intention of making himself king,

> But that necessity so bowed the state
> That I and greatness were compelled to kiss.
> Pt. 2, iii. 1. 73f.

Again in the final scene with his son, the dying usurper speaks as though genuinely believing that his success was unpremeditated. 'It seemed in me,' he tells Hal,

> But as an honour snatched with boist'rous hand;
> Pt. 2, iv. 5. 191

as though he had been a younger Hotspur acting on wild impulse, and not a patiently scheming hypocrite. There is a further surprise in his admission of bewilderment at the working of political forces which have plainly not been in his command. 'God knows, my son,' he says, expressing a perplexity that again seems unassumed,

> By what by-paths and indirect crook'd ways
> I met this crown.

Ibid., 184f.

The crooked ways may have been the course of deceit and concealment which enabled him to outwit both Richard and his own supporters, but there is a sense of puzzled uncertainty in the speech which suggests that events have followed an enigmatic purpose of their own, using Bolingbroke to fulfil purposes which he still does not comprehend. This is probably the significance of his repeated claim to have had no designs on the crown. In his function as character, Bolingbroke embodies an ambition for power which exploited every means of attaining its end, however dishonourable. Only a memory as evasive as his political motives could misrepresent truth so badly as to tell Warwick that he was obliged to assume the crown in the interests of good government. But as a history-play, *Henry IV* is concerned to show the underlying irony of political events, which reverses reasonable hopes in the unforeseen consequences of actions simple enough in themselves. The dying Bolingbroke recognises that his bold crime has not simply established him as king, decisively cutting off the past, but has progressively involved him in unrest and confusion:

> For all my reign hath been but as a scene
> Acting that argument.

Ibid., 197f.

Here Shakespeare gives him a second function not always compatible with that of character. His protestations are not attempts to whitewash his guilt but an expression of

95

bewilderment, in a politician who realises at last that events have determined their own course without respect for his purposes.

The consequences of his crime pass over him unperceived until he is near death. Early in the play he suggests that Hal's shameful reputation may be retribution for some sin of his own, but shows no sense of what his remark implies. 'I know not', he begins, characteristically blind to moral significance,

> whether God will have it so
> For some displeasing service I have done,
> That in his secret doom out of my blood
> He'll breed revengement and a scourge for me.
>
> Pt. 1, iii. 2. 4–7

On the only occasion when Bolingbroke suspects that his troubled reign may be the punishment of some forgotten wrong, he supposes that his son has been sent to afflict him. He has already made one attempt to shift the responsibility for his burdened conscience upon Hal, telling his attendants, 'If any plague hang over us, 'tis he.'[1] His belief is exactly and typically mistaken. His inability to recognise the true source of his own disquiet and of the political unrest of his kingdom is matched by a more ironic failure to acknowledge the parallel between the rebels and himself. As the rebellion gathers head he tells the Prince, 'Even as I was then is Percy now', not realising that he damns himself by the comparison. The irony is renewed when he confronts the rebels before the battle, rebuking Worcester in particular: 'You have betrayed our trust.' His treachery towards Richard and his own accomplices leaves Bolingbroke open to the

[1] *Richard II*, v. 3. 3

96

same accusation, but the point escapes him. Similar undertones of irony develop whenever the King or his spokesmen encounter the rebels. Their lofty moral rebukes are intended to shame the rebels into respect for the sovereignty of law, but in fact they recoil upon the speaker by recalling Bolingbroke's insurrection and condemning his more serious crime. When he refers to Hotspur's baseless assumption of authority, 'of no right, nor colour like to right', the King is unconsciously describing his own lack of legal title, which the rebels regard as 'too indirect for long continuance'. Prince John draws a much finer unobserved parallel during his meeting with the rebel leaders at Gaultree Forest. 'That man that sits within a monarch's heart,' he remarks to the Archbishop,

> And ripens in the sunshine of his favour,
> Would he abuse the countenance of the king,
> Alack, what mischiefs might he set abroach
> In shadow of such greatness!
>
> Pt. 2, iv. 2. 12–15

Bolingbroke had enjoyed none of Richard's royal favour, but the phrase 'abuse the countenance of the king' associates him very closely with the man whom his son is condemning. As a spurious figure of kingship who has taken his sacred office by force, Bolingbroke is abusing the symbol of anointed majesty. The inadvertent sense of rebuke is deepened by what follows. The mischief which most troubles the kingdom, in the upheavals of civil war which Prince John is trying to suppress, has been set on foot by Bolingbroke 'in shadow of such greatness', meaning the royal imposture which has destroyed the authority of settled government. The sense of Prince John's remarks bears still more closely upon Bolingbroke as the Archbishop is attacked as a traitor who would 'misuse the reverence' of his place,

> Employ the countenance and grace of heaven,
> As a false favourite doth his prince's name,
> In deeds dishonourable.
>
> Ibid., 24–26

But the grace of heaven is conferred on kings as well as upon archbishops, and the royal office is invested with still greater sanctity, which Bolingbroke has misused by giving countenance—in the double sense of false face and patronage—to the lawless acts now repeated by the rebels. As before, the moral indictment brought by Bolingbroke's spokesman is most effective in discrediting his own authority, whose basis is implicitly called into question. The King's silence on the moral issues raised by deposing Richard and stealing his crown is broken unconsciously by these scandalised comments on rebellion and abuse of trust, for Bolingbroke cannot invoke moral precept against the supporters whom he has cheated without tacitly accusing himself. Blunt may warn the rebels that

> out of limit and true rule
> You stand against anointed majesty;
>
> Pt. 1, iv. 3. 39f.

but the crime had been greater when the king was true heir to the crown, and Bolingbroke has no just appeal against their attempt to overthrow him.

His kingly manner helps to make his arguments plausible, but throughout *Henry IV* ideas of duplicity and double-dealing are linked with a broader concern with false appearances, leading back to the persistent theme of identity. At Gaultree Forest, Westmoreland acknowledges that the rebels have a plausible case; but he then observes that if rebellion came undisguised and 'like itself'

> in base and abject routs,
> Led on by bloody youth, guarded with rags,
> And countenanced by boys and beggary
> > Pt. 2, iv. 1. 33–35

then the Archbishop and his noble supporters would not have been there,

> to dress the ugly form
> Of base and bloody insurrection
> > Ibid., 39f.

with their honourable names. As spokesman for Boling-broke, Westmoreland is in a weak position to offer such criticism. If everything were to appear 'like itself', Bolingbroke would lose his royal trappings and stand revealed in his true shape as robber and cut-throat. However convincingly he enacts the part of king, the rebels do not allow the fact to drop out of sight that Bolingbroke has no true title to the throne. The political necessity which he pleads—implausibly, if we accept the rebels' account of his calculated deceit—might have been justified by Richard's irresponsibility and misgovern-ment, but usurpation and regicide are blots which darken his majesty irredeemably. The doubtfulness of his royal identity is represented during the battle of Shrewsbury, when Bolingbroke shows his habitual duplicity by sending decoys into the field, wearing his own insignia. The device protects him against Douglas, who dissipates his energy upon a succession of sacrificial counterfeits. When Douglas at last corners him, Bolingbroke disregards the implications of his enemy's question,

> What art thou,
> That counterfeit'st the person of a king?
> > Pt. 1, v. 4. 26f.

99

to answer simply, 'The king himself.' Douglas is not convinced, for while admitting that this new claimant bears himself like a king, he remarks

> I fear thou art another counterfeit.
>
> Ibid., 34

His comment neatly sums up Bolingbroke's equivocal status, as a man having the semblance and manner of a king without the stamp of divine authority. Because Bolingbroke has persuaded himself of his right to rule where only he can provide capable government, he cannot realise that in a deeper sense his assumption of the king's person is an imposture. But although there is nothing hypocritical about his performance, the character which he presents is subtly flawed; and Douglas's unwillingness to believe that he is facing 'the king himself' quietly points this doubtfulness of identity. The issue is reflected again in the phrase 'the countenance of the king', used by Prince John; a term whose precise meanings are often difficult to determine,[1] and which in this play is habitually equivocal. Some of the satirical overtones of Prince John's phrase are taken up in Davy's defence of his friend William Visor, described by Shallow as 'an arrant knave, on my knowledge':

> Yet God forbid, sir, but a knave should have some 'countenance at his friend's request. An honest man, sir, is able to speak for himself, when a knave is not.
>
> Pt. 2, v. 1. 40–42

Under this comedy of rural affairs more serious issues are engaged. Shallow's acquiescence—'Go to, I say he shall have no wrong'—shows how easily justice is perverted under a king who has established himself against ordered

---

[1] See Onions, *A Shakespeare Glossary*, 'countenance'.

principle. In Bolingbroke's kingdom it is appropriate that a knave should 'have some countenance'; though Falstaff seems to think otherwise when he remarks that 'the poor abuses of the time want countenance'. The sense of his comment is more difficult to pin down than Davy's. Its obvious meaning is that rogues are not protected and patronised; a sardonic piece of irony when a usurper is on the throne. Falstaff may be implying that although petty crimes are punished, major criminals like Bolingbroke are countenanced as readily as William Visor of Woncote. A third sense of Falstaff's remark is that villainy goes unmasked, without troubling to disguise its true nature. The ironies of the term are finally compounded at Hal's accession, when Falstaff encourages his companions to 'mark the countenance he will give me', but discovers that the new king has no patronage for crime and lawlessness.

Bolingbroke's reign entails a prolonged struggle to capture the reality of kingship, by adding to his personal dignity and command the invested honour which he could not steal from Richard. The struggle imposes strains upon him which drain his previously buoyant energy and wear him down to the point of exhausted collapse. The opening of the play finds him already 'wan with care', and the unremitting worries of a troubled reign make ravages in his body as well as denying him all mental quiet. 'The incessant care and labour of his mind,' Clarence explains when his father breaks down before his death,

> Hath wrought the mure, that should confine it in,
> So thin that life looks through and will break out.
>
> Pt. 2, iv. 4. 119f.

Emaciated and waxen, he has lost the natural substance

of kingship which gave him so heavy an advantage over Richard. To Bolingbroke it seems that sleeplessness and anxiety are the inescapable lot of the king, and that no sovereign is exempt from the crushing responsibilities which tax human power beyond its limits. 'Thou seek'st the greatness that shall overwhelm thee,' he warns the son who seems impatient for the crown; and although mistaken about Hal's intentions, Bolingbroke is speaking out of his own experience with plain honesty. He still does not understand that the endless disquiet and strain which he has suffered stem from the effort of maintaining a false position, and supplying by force of will the authority divinely implanted in a lawful king. For him majesty has been not so much a dignity as a torment, a crippling and painful burden from which he dare not separate himself:

> Like a rich armour worn in heat of day,
> That scald'st with safety.
>
> Pt. 2, iv. 5. 29f.

Only a usurping king would find the weight of his great office so torturing. Bolingbroke's mind seems unusually awake to images of physical pain. An early allusion to the Redeemer whose feet

> were nailed
> For our advantage on the bitter cross
>
> Pt. 1, i. 1. 26f.

evokes instead of a sense of the redemption which Bolingbroke hopes to obtain, an impression of the sharp discomfort he is suffering. His mental perturbation is shared by Hotspur, who betrays in sleep the guilty agitation excited by his own attempt on the crown. 'Beads of sweat have stood upon thy brow,' Lady Hotspur tells him,

Like bubbles in a late-disturbed stream,
And in thy face strange motions have appear'd,
Such as we see when men restrain their breath
On some great sudden hest.

Pt. 1, ii. 3 60–63

While outwardly and consciously Hotspur is enthusiastically committed to rebellion, the nervous tension of his unconscious mind admits the momentousness of the moral decision he has taken. A similar dichotomy between Bolingbroke's political assurance and the outraged moral being which he has silenced accounts for the unlocated disquiet which deepens as his reign extends. In his soliloquy over his father's crown, Hal recognises that the prize for which Bolingbroke sacrificed a noble reputation has proved a destructive parasite:

The care on thee depending
Hath fed upon the body of my father;
Therefore thou best of gold art worst of gold . . .
Hast eat thy bearer up.

Pt. 2, iv. 5. 158–164

On a usurping head the crown, 'most honoured, most renowned', has lost its medicinal property and feeds like a cancer upon its host. Hal, trying its effects upon him as true inheritor, proves immune to the mad covetousness which took hold of the young Bolingbroke as of other ambitious noblemen of the history-plays. 'If it did infect my blood with joy,' Hal tells his father,

Or swell my thoughts to any strain of pride . . .
Let God forever keep it from my head.

Ibid., 170–4

This lack of response to the personal attractions of kingship, coupled with the reference to his right of inheritance, stands as a tacit condemnation of Bolingbroke which also

103

helps to explain why the crown, although 'best of gold', has consumed him like a wasting disease. He dies broken by his achievement, and gnawed spiritually at the end by the unabsolved guilt of Richard's death. The pilgrimage that was to expiate his crime has been obstructed first by the disturbance that followed his usurpation, and later by his own sickness and frailty which the strain of uneasy rule has brought on. The well-meaning hope of expunging the stain on his possession of the crown is ironically frustrated by the consequences of his crime. Bolingbroke's final reference to this still unforgotten outrage to justice and divine law is a blurred expression of remorse,

> How I came by the crown, O God forgive!
> Ibid., 218

still uncomprehending the design of events which should have assured his triumph. The discovery he makes on his death-bed, of equivocal sense in the prophecy that he 'should not die but in Jerusalem', gives the last ironic twist to the false promises which have led him into a maze. As though in answer to his political double-dealing and the ambiguous position he has occupied, he has been made the victim of a purpose as indirect as his own, and far more cryptic.

Bolingbroke's behaviour in *Henry IV* does not leave an entirely unfavourable impression. The distress which he feels for his kingdom, 'sick with civil blows', may not attract much sympathy, for he is himself responsible for the loss of ordered rule; but this does not affect the sincerity of his concern. That he lacks the power to give England peace and security, and must leave his kingdom to an heir who will foster lawlessness and riot, causes him grief which needs only greater self-awareness to become tragic. He has elements of greatness which outweigh the vicious and dishonourable traits revealed in his unpaid debts, and a sincere wish to bring stable and responsible government to a country almost ruined by Richard's extravagance. These features of his character make it difficult to share the rebels' opinion of Bolingbroke as a thieving hypocrite and cheat, lining his nest at his friends' expense and greedily refusing to share what he has won with their help. But this figure of Bolingbroke cannot be thrust out of the play. However successfully the King conceals his effrontery in counterfeiting the figure of majesty, his grotesque counterpart mocks at this, presenting a farcical parody of the shameful acts and nature which Bolingbroke keeps hidden from himself and the world at large. The disrespectful satirist is Falstaff; a clown whose unofficial function gives him greater liberty than the court fool whose duties he seems to have adopted. He justifies his place in the play not merely by providing comic relief from serious political affairs, but by duplicating in his own shameless behaviour the moral weaknesses of the impostor who claims to personify the king.

II. FALSTAFF

Falstaff crosses Bolingbroke's path only once, and utters only one remark in the royal presence. Before the battle at Shrewsbury he stands with the King's supporters as Worcester makes his accusation of bad faith and sinister purposes, and when Worcester denies that the rebellion is of his seeking, Falstaff throws in a clownish comment answering the King's sceptical question, 'How comes it then?'

Rebellion lay in his way, and he found it.
Pt. I, v. I. 28

Hal prevents any further interjections. The quip characterises Falstaff's function as comic satirist, using ridicule to expose the moral sham which Worcester sets up; but his sarcastic gloss does more than this. When Bolingbroke explains how the pressure of events had forced him to assume the crown, he offers an excuse closely akin to Worcester's. The irreverent thrust which demolishes Worcester's pretence of unwilling participation in armed rebellion disposes in advance of Bolingbroke's argument that he and greatness were 'compelled to kiss'. The incident suggests that Falstaff's bent for destructive satire makes him a dangerous person to leave within earshot of the King. There is probably a further reason why Shakespeare allows these two major characters only this moment of indirect contact.

Falstaff and Bolingbroke are linked in a comic relationship whose nature is indicated during the play-acting scene in which Falstaff impersonates the King. At the most obvious level of appreciation, this is a farcical interlude justified by Hal's need to 'practise an answer' for the approaching audience with his father; but the scene rapidly develops beyond this practical purpose. As Falstaff snatches up impromptu regalia, taking a stool for his throne, a cushion as crown, and a dagger as makeshift sceptre, he presents more than a merely clownish figure of barnstorming majesty. The parody relates specifically to Bolingbroke, whose character Falstaff has assumed; and these comic properties have a satirical point as sharp as the dagger which this alehouse king clutches as his badge of authority. The usurper whose crimes have debased the dignity of his royal office enjoys as much right to crown and throne as Falstaff's makeshift properties suggest, and he too guards his stolen property with a ready knife. Yet despite this illicit possession of Richard's crown and the naked show of force, the King maintains an outward majesty which Falstaff parodies in his comic stateliness and aplomb:

> Harry, I do not only marvel where thou spendest thy time, but also how thou art accompanied. For though the camomile, the more it is trodden on the faster it grows, yet youth, the more it is wasted the sooner it wears.
>
> Pt. 1, ii. 4. 393-397

The speech provides a passable forecast of the rebuke to come. Falstaff has briefly taken over the responsibilities as well as the person of Hal's father, and is admonishing riot and disorder in his adopted son with a complete—and comic—lack of moral right; being far more dissolute himself. However ludicrous its exterior form, Falstaff's play bears the same relationship to the events and characters it represents as drama to life generally, showing their true nature with the help of illusion and pretence. This farcically disrespectful imposture by Falstaff gives visible form to the moral reality of Bolingbroke's kingship, and supplies in advance a satirical commentary on the gravely serious scene between Hal and his father.

The moral force of the parody is strengthened by Falstaff's unashamed recommendation of himself as a proper companion for the Prince. Describing an entirely illusory self—'a virtuous man whom I have often noted'—he seems to lose sight of his dramatic role in the relish of his approval:

> A goodly portly man, i' faith, and a corpulent; of a cheerful look, a pleasing eye, and a most noble carriage ... If that

man should be lewdly given, he deceiveth me; for, Harry, I
see virtue in his looks.

Ibid., 416–22

There is no self-deception, for Falstaff knows and acknowledges his moral frailties with comic unconcern, and is
here making a joke of his scandalous levity. The comedy
of the speech is intensified by the fact that pseudo-
Bolingbroke is speaking. If the King were to describe his
own moral character, the portrait would not be as flatter-
ing; but it would probably be as indulgent and blind to
faults as Falstaff is pretending to be towards the 'goodly
portly man' who is Hal's constant companion. For
Bolingbroke to approve of his son's association with
Falstaff would be inconceivable; but there is some
justice in Falstaff's suggestion, in the kingly character
which he assumes, that Hal should submit himself to this
virtuous influence. The embodiment of riot is a fit
associate for the son of a usurper, though Bolingbroke
does not recognise the appropriateness. How far Falstaff
sinks himself in his part is not clear, but however absurdly
he seems to reverse the actual arguments and attitudes of
Bolingbroke, he in fact maintains close contact with the
moral reality of his royal double; and acts out in bald and
irreverent terms the disgraced and ignoble figure from
whom Bolingbroke has almost dissociated himself.

This comic duplication, which Falstaff assigns to
some of the characteristic functions of the Fool, raises a
large problem of interpretation. Is the often wildly
disrespectful, point-blank moral judgement which Falstaff presents, or enacts, to be accepted as truth? The
question proposes itself in respect of other plays, and
most conspicuously in *King Lear*. Mother-wit and almost
painfully sharp discernment enable the Fool to seize

upon essential feelings that are smothered by hypocrisy or cunning, and to this extent to make a true analysis of character. But the expression of his truth involves a comic reduction of scale, a representation of the majestic in terms of the homely, which seems to introduce the distortion of caricature. A similar difficulty attaches to Falstaff's satirical doubling. The grotesque dissolute figure who dogs Bolingbroke's footsteps, or parodies his imposing show of royal dignity, may be merely exploiting discreditable features of the King's character, unjustly bringing obloquy upon the whole man. But it seems more likely that Falstaff's satirical function is to counterpoise the forgetfulness that allows Bolingbroke to give so plausible a performance as king. Falstaff's comically distorted allusions to wrongs committed by Bolingbroke against Richard, his own supporters, and the laws of which he is now supreme protector, keep the audience awake to the irrevocable dishonour which the King has incurred, and frustrate his attempts to pass himself off as the authentic figure of God's deputy-elect.

The comic parallel begins to be drawn with the earliest low-life scenes, where preparations for the Gad's Hill robbery call in references to theft and fraud. The robbery is manifestly a comically scaled-down version of Boling-broke's original crime, followed by a matching sequel in which a group of fellow-conspirators attempt to snatch the booty from their successful partners; incidentally revealing the cowardice of the original thief. Although not a crown, the prize is royal gold; 'money of the King's . . . going to the King's exchequer'; and thus this crime too involves an interception of appointed right, designed to give the thieves wrongful possession of the king's property by force. Promises of sharing the prize, and at least one scornfully mistrustful rejection of this verbal pledge, develop ideas introduced during the quarrel between Bolingbroke and the Percies in the first act of the play and repeated in later scenes. 'Thou shalt have a share in our purchase, as I am a true man,' Gadshill promises, but the Chamberlain asks for a less equivocal assurance:

> Nay, rather let me have it as you are a false thief.
>
> Pt. 1, ii. 1. 92

The overtones of these linked terms touch sympathetic chords in the political scenes of the play. The remark made by Falstaff when his confederates leave him to struggle for himself is appropriate in either context:

> A plague upon't when thieves cannot be true one to another!
>
> Pt. 1, ii. 2. 27f.

But as the Chamberlain recognises, a thief cannot be a true man, having dishonest intentions as well as a false face, and neither Falstaff nor Hotspur should expect just dealings of an associate who has proved his contempt for 'truth' by participating in robbery. The term 'truth' now includes the further sense of fidelity, and recalls the oath of loyalty to Richard which Bolingbroke dishonoured. He has failed to behave like a true man in the sense applied by the Prince in commenting on the robbers' treatment of the travellers, 'The thieves have bound the true men'; meaning the loyal subjects who were carrying the King's money. His comment looks towards the moral topsy-turveydom of Bolingbroke's rule, where the administration is in the hands of a robber. When Falstaff remarks that 'the true prince may, for recreation sake, prove a false thief', he is addressing Hal; but apparently looking towards the throne.

Unlike Falstaff, Bolingbroke foils his fellow-conspirators' attempt to dispossess him. In this respect the parallel between the two lines of action breaks down. But the double robbery at Gad's Hill, placed immediately after the first movings of political conspiracy, represents the rebels' purpose in a ludicrous form which brings its moral contradictions to light. At this stage of their plot the rebels speak regretfully of their betrayal of Richard, 'that sweet lovely rose', and seem bent upon redeeming the honourable reputations lost in aiding Bolingbroke, by setting Mortimer on the throne. Little more is heard about these good intentions. When they meet to sign the indentures, the rebels are taken up with the more pressing business of dividing the spoils which they have still to win, and with quarrelling among themselves about equality of shares. The pretence of enforcing justice has been abandoned, and the bare purpose of robbing a thief and embezzler is no longer seriously disguised. The farcical double robbery can then be appreciated as a true moral counterpart of Hotspur's attempt to seize Bolingbroke's stolen crown, where both rebel and usurper profess lofty and disinterested motives for outraging law and a private undertaking.

As a further point of difference between these parallel forms of the same crime, the money stolen at Gad's Hill is returned to its owners. The immediate significance of Hal's action is to prove his dissociation from the criminal instincts of both political factions, but it also brings to light a characteristic which Falstaff shares with Bolingbroke. When he learns that the money has been repaid, Falstaff is crestfallen:

> O, I do not like that paying back, 'tis a double labour.
> > Pt. i, iii. 3. 178f.

His debts are a comic issue of both parts of *Henry IV*. In the third tavern scene of Part 1 he brings a trumped-up charge against his hostess of harbouring pickpockets in the house, with motives which she is quick to recognise:

> You owe me money, Sir John, and now you pick a quarrel to beguile me of it.
>
> Ibid., 64f.

She has a truer intuition than the rebels, who fail to perceive that Bolingbroke deliberately sows discord between himself and them for the same reason. The general parallel becomes suddenly more specific as Quickly mentions some items of Falstaff's debt, 'a dozen of shirts to your back', besides twenty-four pounds in ready money. The suggestion of threadbare poverty, relieved only to be scornfully denied—'Dowlas, filthy dowlas'—offers a ludicrous counterpart to Bolingbroke's ingratitude towards the friends who gave him 'that same majesty he wears' at a time when he was destitute, 'a poor unminded outlaw sneaking home'. Falstaff remains brazenly defiant in the face of Quickly's reminder, refusing to pay a denier but at least admitting a past obligation, where Bolingbroke declines to notice the impeachment. Hotspur's bitter comment rebukes his own credulity as much as Bolingbroke's bad faith:

> The King is kind, and well we know the King
> Knows at what time to promise, when to pay.
>
> Pt. 1, iv. 3. 52f.

The remark is half-way to the indirect satire which Falstaff enacts in his own attempt to evade his debt. His impudent retort to his accuser matches the accusation of wrongful proceeding brought by the King's spokesmen, condemning the rebels for faults more glaringly obvious in their master:

> There's no more faith in thee than in a stewed prune, nor no more truth in thee than in a drawn fox—and for womanhood, Maid Marian may be the deputy's wife of the ward to thee.
>
> Pt. I, iii. 3. 110–13

Hal intervenes with a moral rebuke of Falstaff's lying and duplicity which shows his air of personal consequence to be so much worthless stuffing:

> There's no room for faith, truth, nor honesty in this bosom of thine—it is all filled up with guts and midriff . . . If there were anything in thy pocket but tavern-reckonings, memorandums of bawdy-houses, and one poor pennyworth of sugar-candy to make thee long-winded . . . I am a villain.
>
> Ibid., 152–61

Falstaff is carrying out his satirical function by behaving in a fashion which encourages the Prince to castigate him in terms appropriate to Bolingbroke. This is not the only occasion, in either part of the play, when Hal seems to be tacitly denouncing his father's viciousness by attacking the same faults in Falstaff. This means of registering moral disapproval of Bolingbroke's crimes indirectly allows the Prince to dissociate himself completely from a lawless régime without overt disloyalty to his father. When we realise that Falstaff is unwittingly standing-in for the man whose moral character he shares, we may feel less uneasy about the gratuitousness of Hal's sometimes scathing attacks upon Falstaff, whose company he is not obliged to tolerate. The vehemence of his personal insults—'that bolting-hutch of beastliness, that swollen parcel of dropsies . . . that stuffed cloak-bag of guts'—

H 113

springs partly from moral disgust, but perhaps more from the frustration of being denied any direct outlet for this revulsion. At such moments Falstaff becomes the scapegoat for Bolingbroke, and the target of a satirical venom whose shafts are often ambiguously appropriate to both. This ambiguousness is particularly evident in Hal's speech from the throne denouncing

> that reverend vice, that grey iniquity, that father ruffian.
> Pt. 1, ii. 4. 447f.

His satirical terms fit Bolingbroke rather better than Falstaff. Sir John may deserve 'reverend vice' for his jocular pretence of respectability, but the King—a crowned robber, holding sacred office in defiance of right—has a stronger claim to the description. The second epithet applies to both without distinction; but 'that father ruffian' must indicate Bolingbroke rather than Falstaff, if only because 'your father' is a common form of reference to the King in the tavern scenes. Falstaff may be a father ruffian in the sense that he embodies riot and misrule, but the description applies to Bolingbroke in a literal as well as a figurative sense, as the speaker has best reason to know. The indictment of Falstaff cannot be transferred entirely to the King, as though he and not Falstaff were being charged, but the terms of Hal's speech are equivocal enough to suggest some merging of their individual identities, allowing one to be seen as a variant form of the other.

Falstaff's debt to his hostess remains unpaid at the beginning of Part 2, where his exasperated creditor has called in the law and arranged for him to be arrested. Her warning to the officers throws some unexpected light on Falstaff's character:

Take heed of him, he stabbed me in mine own house, most beastly in good faith. A' cares not what mischief he does, if his weapon be out; he will foin like any devil.

Pt. 2, ii. 1. 13–16

There is some sexual *double entendre* here—much, perhaps; for neither at Gad's Hill nor at Shrewsbury does Falstaff show any fondness for close-quarter fighting. Quickly must be mistaken, but her warning recalls the play-scene and the dagger in the player king's hand; and the attempt to bring a well-armed and dangerous debtor to justice takes on a deeper significance. All the main features of the rebels' complaint against Bolingbroke recur in comic form: the accusation of bad faith and double-dealing, the repudiation of a debt long overdue for payment, and the angry determination of the creditor to exact full satisfaction. 'I have borne, and borne, and borne,' Quickly declares,

and have been fubbed off, and fubbed off, and fubbed off, from this day to that day, that it is a shame to be thought on. There is no honesty in such dealing.

Ibid., 32–35

On this occasion not Hal but the Lord Chief Justice intervenes, and the plaintiff is encouraged to extend her accusations by charging Falstaff with greed and misappropriation; still duplicating the rebels' grievances:

He hath eaten me out of house and home, he hath put all my substance into that fat belly of his. But I will have some of it out again, or I will ride thee a-nights like the mare.

Ibid., 72–75

The fact that Bolingbroke is not physically corpulent does not obstruct the parallel. When Worcester speaks of the rebels' part in making him 'portly' he suggests that the

King is swollen with the proceeds of his robbery as well as with self-importance. The suggestion is put much more plainly when Worcester describes Bolingbroke as an insatiable cuckoo—the idea of unlawful intrusion has its own relevance—who

> Grew by our feeding to so great a bulk
> That even our love durst not come near your sight
> For fear of swallowing.
>
> Pt. I, v. I. 62–64

The images compel us to see Bolingbroke, if only for a moment, as a figure with the grossness of Falstaff; a 'huge hill of flesh'. Having gorged himself at his supporters' expense, cuckoo-Bolingbroke is as obese and distended as the 'stuffed cloak-bag of guts' whom Hal savagely abuses, and open to the same disgusted condemnation. The vengeful promise to 'have some of it out again' voiced by Falstaff's hostess puts in bald terms the rebels' determination to recover by force what the King owes them, or like Quickly to plague him with unrest.

The Lord Chief Justice finds for the plaintiff, and censures the impudence in Falstaff that has driven his creditor to take extreme measures:

> Are you not ashamed to enforce a poor widow to so rough a course to come by her own?
>
> Pt. 2, ii. I. 8of.

The rebuke picks up the rebels' argument that a resort to violence has been forced upon them by Bolingbroke's intransigence, and leads to the disclosure that Falstaff owes his hostess himself as well as money and goods. 'Thou didst swear to me,' Quickly reminds him with a wealth of circumstantial detail,

upon a parcel-gilt goblet, sitting in my Dolphin-chamber at
the round table, by a sea-coal fire, upon Wednesday in Wheeson
week . . . to marry me, and make me my lady thy wife.
Canst thou deny it?

Ibid., 84–91

Bolingbroke is reminded of his act of perjury in less
detailed terms, and Worcester makes no use of the telling
fact that his oath had been 'receiued vpon the euangelists';
but the general similarity of the two accusations shows
how closely the low-life comedy shadows its grander
counterpart. 'You swore to us,' Worcester recalls,

> And you did swear that oath at Doncaster,
> That you did nothing purpose 'gainst the state,
> Nor claim no further than your new-fall'n right,
> The seat of Gaunt, dukedom of Lancaster.

Pt. 1, v. 1. 42–45

Bolingbroke does not try to refute the accusation, but
falls back upon kingly hauteur and speaks contemptu-
ously of the rebels' efforts to attract support through this
charge, dismissing their adherents as 'fickle changelings
and poor discontents'. Falstaff attempts to discredit his
hostess's impeachment by the same means, explaining,
'My lord, this is a poor mad soul'; but his judge is not
taken in. 'You have, as it appears to me,' he tells Falstaff,

> practised upon the easy-yielding spirit of this woman, and
> made her serve your uses both in purse and in person . . . Pay
> her the debt you owe her, and unpay the villainy you have
> done with her. The one you may do with sterling money, and
> the other with current repentance.

Pt. 2, ii. 1. 112–20

The stipulation 'sterling money' is a necessary one in a
kingdom where counterfeiting is so common. In the

117

related episode of Part 1, the moral rebuke of Falstaff's lying and duplicity is uttered by Hal, a spokesman whose ambiguous position qualifies the force of the check. In contrast the Lord Chief Justice is a morally un-assailable figure who descends into the doubtful world of Quickly's customers to confront Falstaff with an indictment which cannot be deflected by a bribe or a jest. In Eastcheap, and involved in the complaint of a cheated tavern-keeper, the Lord Chief Justice seems incongruously out of place; but it is only here that he can meet and admonish the representative figure of riot and lawlessness, whose unreproved crime brings the whole institution of justice into disrepute. As Falstaff's misdeeds are a petty form of Bolingbroke's political embezzling, in rebuking Falstaff the Lord Chief Justice makes an indirect attack upon the far more serious crimes committed by the King, which only the rebels condemn to his face. Under the rule of a usurper, justice can express itself only obliquely; but in this scene its symbolic figure contrives to speak out sharply and unequivocally against the wrongs which still go unpunished in Bolingbroke.

Falstaff's unwillingness to acknowledge any form of debt manifests itself again on the battlefield at Shrewsbury, where he finds himself at uncomfortably close quarters with a creditor who will not be put off with promises. In London, he admits, he could escape shot-free,[1] but on the battlefield there is 'no scoring but upon the pate'. When Hal reminds him that he owes God a death, Falstaff answers characteristically:

> 'Tis not due yet. I would be loath to pay him before his day.
> Pt. 1, v. 1. 127f.

---

[1] (i) unwounded, (ii) without paying the reckoning.

Acting on this principle, he finds no difficulty either in adopting the ignominious ruse of shamming dead in the face of danger, or in justifying his cowardice afterwards. ''Twas time to counterfeit,' he explains,

> or that hot termagant Scot had paid me, scot and lot too.
> Pt. 1, v. 4. 112f.

But the term 'counterfeit' presents a moral challenge to the position he has taken up, and to silence the imputation of unworthy behaviour he turns the tables on the word:

> Counterfeit? I lie, I am no counterfeit: to die is to be a counterfeit, for he is but the counterfeit of a man who hath not the life of a man: but to counterfeit dying when a man thereby liveth is to be no counterfeit, but the true and perfect image of life indeed.
>
> Ibid., 114–19

His argument might interest Bolingbroke, who has a similar concern to prove himself no counterfeit, and a still more cogent affinity with Falstaff in his anxiety to escape the Douglas. The King adopts a different form of the same ruse, sending decoys into battle wearing the royal surcoat, and sheltering behind friends who are killed in mistake for himself. Beneath his majestic bearing, the cowardly instinct of self-preservation baldly revealed in Falstaff motivates Bolingbroke just as powerfully; but without Falstaff's indirectly satirical comment the ignobility of the King's stratagem might pass unnoticed. The point is made more plainly when Falstaff comes across the dead body of Blunt, one of the counterfeits sacrificed to protect Bolingbroke from his enemy, and repudiates the noble reputation which puts life into hazard:

I like not such grinning honour as Sir Walter hath. Give me
life, which if I can save, so; if not, honour comes unlooked-
for.

Pt. 1, v. 3. 58–61

Evidently Bolingbroke shares this view. Already dishonoured by the deposition and murder of his cousin, his
chief purpose at Shrewsbury is not to redeem himself by
courageously fighting, but to survive the battle as victor.
Like so many of Falstaff's actions and comments, the
catechism of honour which seems to typify his own
shameless outlook puts in plain terms the principles
underlying Bolingbroke's behaviour:

What is honour? a word. What is in that word honour? What
is that honour? Air. A trim reckoning! Who hath it? He
that died a-Wednesday.

Pt. 1, v. 1. 134–6

Of all the combatants at Shrewsbury, only the King and
his grotesque counterpart try to save their own skins;
both of them by means of the counterfeiting that is so
deeply characteristic of Bolingbroke. Hotspur, the Prince,
and the other combatants throw themselves whole-
heartedly into the battle, as though calling attention to the
King's reluctance to expose himself in a fight to determine his own authority. The catechism of honour is not
directed satirically against Hotspur's rapturous ideal of
knighthood

O gentlemen, the time of life is short!
To spend that shortness basely were too long
Pt. 1, v. 2. 81f.

or against Hal's more sober respect for noble reputation.
Its target is Bolingbroke. Falstaff is himself of course
involved in the satirical consequences of his defence of

cowardice, but knowingly; making himself ridiculous by the deliberate sophistry of his argument in order to reveal the unspoken, unadmitted purpose which prompts Bolingbroke's ruse.

Over the body of Hotspur, with the promise of a noble reputation stolen from his friend Hal, Falstaff promises a reformation that will be physical as well as moral. 'If I do grow great, I'll grow less,' he tells himself,

> for I'll purge, and leave sack, and live cleanly as a nobleman should do.
>
> Pt. i, v. 4. 163f.

His play on words reveals the double impulse that will bring this promised improvement to nothing. It will not be the first time that his good intentions have collapsed. At his first appearance in the play he comes on stage moodily penitent, admitting himself little better than one of the wicked, and wishing he knew 'where a commodity of good names were to be bought'. Then, in a sudden burst of resolution, he decides to make a complete break with the disreputable life of Eastcheap:

> I must give over this life, and I will give it over: by the Lord, and I do not I am a villain.
>
> Pt. i, i. 2. 93f.

His penitent mood barely outlives this resolution. Hal has only to ask, with seeming irrelevance, where they are to steal their next purse, to recall Falstaff to his natural vocation. If he does not bear a hand, Falstaff asserts, they may call him a villain and baffle him: a means of degrading a perjured knight by hanging him upside-down. The punishment is obviously more appropriate to Bolingbroke, whose associations with theft and perjury remain a major issue with the rebels. Falstaff's spiritual misgivings have evidently lasted for some time before this sudden change of mood. Poins, coming in immediately afterwards, greets Falstaff as 'Monsieur Remorse', and jokes about the misdeed which he supposes to be troubling Falstaff's conscience:

> Jack, how agrees the devil and thee about thy soul, that thou soldest to him on Good Friday last for a cup of Madeira and a cold capon's leg?
>
> Ibid., 111–13

The underlying significance of this uncharacteristic melancholy, and of Poins's flippant question, are suggested by the parallels which they draw with the previous scene. Falstaff's depression provides a comic echo of Bolingbroke's careworn anxiety, and his resolution to 'give it over' is a disrespectful parody of the King's renewed plan to visit the Holy Land, first announced after the murder of Richard. The allusion to Good Friday in Poins's speech seems to pick up Bolingbroke's reference to the Crucifixion in the scene just ended; and to connect more distantly with the political Good Friday of Richard's betrayal:

> You Pilates
> Have here delivered me to my sour cross,
> And water cannot wash away your sin.
>
> R II, iv. 1. 240–2

Bolingbroke's leading part in this crime has brought him a more substantial reward than the comic parallel suggests, but Poins indicates both the greed which motivated him and the uneasiness which has ensued. Hal assures Poins that the compact will be respected: 'Sir John stands to his word, the devil shall have his bargain'; and there follows some word-play about promise-keeping and giving the devil his due which has ominous overtones for those who habitually default on their creditors.

The shadow of unquiet conscience falls across Falstaff from time to time, to be put aside with wistful recollection of lost innocence, and accepted as a discomfort as inevitable and as transient as indigestion. 'A plague of sighing and grief!' he exclaims in the second tavern scene, 'It blows a man up like a bladder.' It is a novel way of accounting for corpulence, and admits the shallowness of Falstaff's anxieties. When the sheriff and his men invade the tavern after the Gad's Hill robbery, and the Prince calls for 'a true face and a good conscience', Falstaff acknowledges with complete aplomb that he can supply neither:

> Both of which I have had, but their date is out, and therefore I'll hide me.
>
> Pt. i, ii. 4. 496f.

But when he next appears he makes it appear that his worries have now begun to eat into him. 'Do I not dwindle?' he asks Bardolph. 'Why, my skin hangs about me like an old lady's loose gown. I am withered like an old apple-john.' This loss of substance induces another burst of penitent resolution:

> Well, I'll repent, and that suddenly, while I am in some liking . . . And I have not forgotten what the inside of a church is made of, I am a peppercorn, a brewer's horse . . . Company, villainous company, hath been the spoil of me.
>
> Pt. i, iii. 3. 4–10

Bardolph concurs in the diagnosis: 'You are so fretful you cannot live long'; but Falstaff is not disposed to treat his condition very seriously, and calls for music, 'a

bawdy song, make me merry'. The idea that he is suffering from a wasting sickness, likely to prove fatal, is merely
clownish; but again Falstaff is acting as comic index to
the increasingly dangerous state of Bolingbroke's moral
and physical health. The parallel with this exchange of
medical opinions lies at some distance, near the end of the
second part of *Henry IV*, and clearly too remote to be
picked up in performance. Its likeness is none the less
striking. Warwick attempts to reassure the Princes after
the King's breakdown, by reminding them that 'these
fits Are with his highness very ordinary'. But this
admission reveals the deadly gravity of their father's
condition, and Clarence echoes Bardolph's opinion of his
master:

> No, no, he cannot long hold out these pangs.
> Pt. 2, iv. 4. 117

The King is moved to another room, where he recovers
sufficiently to ask for music. This seems to parallel
Falstaff's request for a bawdy song to dispel the melancholy of his fatal illness, in the third tavern scene of
Part 1. These episodes too are widely separated, but as
Shakespeare must have known Holinshed's account of
the King's sudden illness and death when he wrote Part 1,
their relationship is not out of the question. The salient
points of the two scenes correspond closely enough,
in their comic mockery of remorse and failing health,
to suggest that Falstaff is again enacting a satirical parody
of Bolingbroke.

When Falstaff reappears at the beginning of Part 2,
unreformed and impenitent, he is no longer making a
comic pretence of being ill, but marked by diseases which
he does his best to ignore. His page brings a warning

from the physician that Falstaff 'might have moe diseases than he knew for'; but his master turns a deaf ear to the report, and takes upon himself the task of diagnosing the King's complaint:

> This apoplexy, as I take it, is a kind of lethargy, and't please your lordship, a kind of sleeping in the blood . . . I have read the cause of his effects in Galen; it is a kind of deafness.
>
> Pt. 2, i. 2. 110–16

The general parallel between Falstaff and Bolingbroke as diseased and ageing men, and between the King and his unhealthy realm, is too plain to be overlooked. The association goes well beyond this general likeness. When the Lord Chief Justice remarks that Falstaff and the King seem to be troubled with the same complaint, Falstaff makes the nice distinction that it is 'the disease of not listening, the malady of not marking', that he suffers from; which confirms their kinship. The moral 'sleeping in the blood' which Falstaff represents in broad physical terms by unbuttoning after supper and sleeping on benches after noon is the manifestation of a spiritual deafness. Similarly in Bolingbroke the 'lethargy' diagnosed by Falstaff is not only physical; and the 'kind of deafness' which afflicts him is a bodily counterpart of his stifling of conscience and disregard of moral law. By admitting his own malady of not marking, Falstaff draws their single identity more closely about himself and the King, making it difficult to separate the two characters into distinct beings. For this reason, every reference to Falstaff's increasing age and ill-health takes on an ambiguous significance, as though spreading beyond its explicit object and impelling attention towards a second figure, sensed rather than seen in the half-light behind him.

The advance of old age presents a second warning which Falstaff ignores like the first. 'You are as a candle, the better part burnt out,' the Lord Chief Justice observes; but Falstaff mocks his heavy sobriety by the staggering assertion that he lost his voice 'with hallooing and singing of anthems', and by remarking that he had a white head 'and something a round belly' at birth. By running circles round his unsmiling opponent Falstaff emerges with honour from the rhetorical contest, but in refusing to acknowledge his advanced age Falstaff is being more than impish. His claim to represent youth sternly repressed by the old, first heard during the attack on the travellers at Gad's Hill, contains an implicit demand for the moral licence granted to young men out of consideration for the natural impulsiveness of youth. Worcester realises that the King will extend this indulgence to Hotspur, though not to himself:

> My nephew's trespass may be well forgot,
> It hath the excuse of youth and heat of blood.
> Pt. 1, v. 2. 16f.

Bolingbroke, who recognises his younger self in Hotspur and speaks of his stolen crown as 'an honour snatched with boisterous hand', appears to be making a tacit plea for the privilege of youth in respect of his own crime. This is the point towards which the satire of Falstaff's preposterous claim to youthfulness is directed. As a man rapidly approaching the grave it behoves Falstaff to amend his dissolute habits without delay, and to prepare himself for his end. It is the wilfulness of this refusal which scandalises the Lord Chief Justice:

> Is not your voice broken, your wind short, your chin double, your wit single, and every part about you blasted with

antiquity? And will you yet call yourself young? Fie, fie, fie,
Sir John!

Pt. 2, i. 2. 181–5

The parallel with Bolingbroke is exact. His crime might
have been prompted by the unreckoning bravado of a
young man, but the ageing usurper whom he has become
cannot expect this face to excuse him now. Repentance
and restitution are overdue, and time is pressing. To some
extent Bolingbroke is physically prevented from absolving
his guilt by the consequences of his crime; but his
remorse is mixed with a determination to cling to his
stolen crown. In the event, Bolingbroke will find no way
of squaring his conscience, and will go wild into his grave;
Hal's phrase suggesting the unpurged character of riot
which, like Falstaff, he maintains to the end.

Although seemingly blind to his own desperate condition, the King is uncomfortably awake to the unhealthy
state of his kingdom;

> How foul it is, what rank diseases grow—
> And with what danger—near the heart of it.
>
> Pt. 2, iii. 1. 39f.

Warwick is at hand with affable assurances, arguing that
the realm is rather 'but as a body yet distempered',

> Which to his former strength may be restored
> With good advice and little medicine.
>
> Ibid., 42f.

His soothing opinion does more credit to Warwick's
diplomacy than to his political acumen. The kingdom is
gravely disordered, and must continue to stand in deadly
peril so long as Bolingbroke's success encourages new
rebels to follow his lawless example. The moral and
physical health of the King are bound up with the state

127

of his realm, and here too only drastic measures offer an effective remedy to the disease which runs on unchecked. The good advice and little medicine recommended by Warwick might prove a temporary palliative, but no cure. Poins supplies a more forthright diagnosis: 'Marry, the immortal part needs a physician, but that moves him not'; and although directed at Falstaff, the remark has the secondary significance that we come to expect of such comments. Falstaff is not entirely proof against reminders of his mortality, as he shows when Doll chides him affectionately:

> When wilt thou leave fighting o' days and foining o' nights, and begin to patch up thine old body for heaven?
>
> Pt. 2, ii. 4. 228–30

Her question unwittingly seeks out the King, a man far more preoccupied than Falstaff with 'fighting o' days', and pressed by a more urgent need to prepare himself for death. In thrusting Doll's warning away from him, Falstaff is speaking for Bolingbroke as well as for himself:

> Peace, good Doll! Do not speak like a death's-head, do not bid me remember mine end.
>
> Ibid., 231f.

The same disinclination to give heed to the approach of death is shown by Shallow, who as a corrupt justice claiming 'some authority' under Bolingbroke has reason to model himself on his royal master. No more disposed than Falstaff to assume the gravity expected of an old man, Shallow continues to re-live the wild exploits of youth which Falstaff, in his simpler satirical function, exposes as senile lies:

> Jesu, Jesu, the mad days that I have spent! And to see how many of my old acquaintance are dead!
>
> Pt. 2, iii. 2. 32–34

The corollary to his reminiscence of misspent youth awakes no anxiety for himself. In common with Falstaff and the King he ignores the shadow lying across his path, paying lip-service to death by uttering sententious platitudes while eagerly watching the market:

> Death, as the psalmist saith, is certain to all; all shall die. How a good yoke of bullocks at Stamford fair?
> > Ibid., 36–38

Again the warning is missed. Shallow himself is on the verge of the grave, but too irrevocably committed to the world of material profit and loss to set his spiritual affairs in order. Recollections of the *bona roba* Jane Nightwork, who fifty-five years after the event 'cannot but be old', press the same tacit warning upon each of the old men in whom Bolingbroke's sins of youth are comically reflected, but meet the same unresponsiveness in them all. When Falstaff tells one of his recruits immediately before these reminiscences,

> Mouldy, it is time you were spent;
> > Ibid., 116f.

it is hard to restrict the expanding sense of his remark to this single figure. The King too, diseased and exhausted by the cares of office, is coming to the end of his resources.

The rebels have already reached this conclusion independently. Hastings finds encouragement for their purposes in Bolingbroke's sickness and his limited means:

> So is the unfirm king
> In three divided, and his coffers sound
> With hollow poverty and emptiness.
> > Pt. 2, i. 3. 73–75

This report follows less than a hundred lines after

Falstaff's page has found only 'seven groats and two pence' in his master's purse. Falstaff's frank comment on his desperate efforts to avoid bankruptcy forms a comic prelude to the account of Bolingbroke's financial straits in the next scene:

> I can get no remedy against this consumption of the purse; borrowing only lingers and lingers it out, but the disease is incurable.
>
> Pt. 2, i. 2. 237–239

The metaphor of an incurable disease has a special appropriateness. Falstaff's 'consumption of the purse' is the counterpart of Bolingbroke's empty coffers, and in both men the approach of bankruptcy after a lifetime of unpaid debts and extended credit is symbolic of an exhausted spiritual exchequer. Although frequently postponed, the final reckoning cannot be evaded. Falstaff evidently hopes to escape critical scrutiny at the end, for he tells the Lord Chief Justice,

> I hope he that looks upon me will take me without weighing.
>
> Pt. 2, i. 2. 164f.

But the opening of a new reign brings him up short against an implacable judgement, and the lingering disease of his insolvency ends as he is carried off to a debtors' prison. The admission to Shallow, 'I owe you a thousand pound', shows us a dazed Falstaff who for the first time acknowledges a debt; a crushing sum which he and his creditor realise can never now be repaid.

Thus Falstaff's satirical function ends with the enacting, through his arrest and committal, of the spiritual fate which has already overtaken the royal figure whom he has parodied. The officers who seize the old, diseased and morally bankrupt Falstaff and drag him off to prison not only personify agents of Tudor justice, but enact a scene in direct descent from Morality tradition. The figure of Vice—here a combination of sloth, gluttony, avarice, lechery and drunkenness— has rejected wholesome counsel and made a mock of penitence, is sentenced by inexorable Justice and carried off by devils to suffer the torments of the damned. Through this final comic interlude Falstaff's association with Bolingbroke, which has persisted during both parts of the play, offers its last oblique suggestion. The King has died with his pilgrimage unperformed and his great crime unabsolved, carrying into the grave a weight of sin which he recognises in telling the Prince,

> All the soil of the achievement goes
> With me into the earth.
> > Pt. 2, iv. 5. 189f.

When the new King speaks of a father who has gone 'wild into his grave' he means, at the simplest level of interpretation, that his own riotousness is buried with Bolingbroke. Other meanings are involved, which suggest the King's agony of spirit as he dies with his guilt still unpurged. The arrest of Falstaff brings to an end a parallel career of infamy and misrule in a form which, behind its low comedy, hints ominously at the spiritual reckoning to which Bolingbroke has been summoned. The hour which both men struggled to put off has at last struck, and a long overdue account has been brought to settlement.

III. THE PRINCE

Unlike the truly profligate Falstaff, Prince Hal has few friends among critics of the play. His popularity is readily accountable. A lone wolf playing a double game to which not even his anxious father is admitted, he is seen waiting to acquire moral estimation by humiliating an old friend in the moment of triumph, and to hoodwink his subjects by a sham reformation prepared well in advance. His behaviour has attracted understandably scornful criticism; and the acknowledgement that this cynical opportunist is to become the dauntless Harry of Harfleur and Agincourt has only added puzzlement to the distaste of readers who cannot forgive his callous deception of Falstaff. The protracted subterfuge which brings him undeserved credit at the expense of his friend's feelings suggests a calculating deceitfulness, much more difficult to condone than Falstaff's implausible impostures or the King's counterfeiting of regal authority.

The difficulty of explaining Hal's actions in terms of human character has to be admitted. There are Shakespearian figures whose behaviour is determined to an appreciable extent by the imaginative design of the play, without first regard to their human plausibility. The Prince is one of them. The incompleteness of his human motivation is at once evident in Shakespeare's vague and contradictory suggestions of what moves Hal to abandon Westminster for Eastcheap and to choose riotous companions, concealing his true character until the time is ripe to disclose himself. The Prince himself prefers to be obscure about his motives, and it is left to Warwick to suggest that good may eventually spring out of this unprincely association with drabs and cutpurses, whose memory

> Shall as a pattern or a measure live
> By which his grace must mete the lives of others,
> Turning past evils to advantages.
>
> Pt. 2, iv. 4. 76–78

The argument does not convince Bolingbroke, but in

Henry V the reformed Hal adapts it to his own use, remarking that the Dauphin fails to grasp the purpose of those 'wilder days',

> Not measuring what use we made of them.
> *Henry V.*, i. 2. 268

Shakespeare's reader must be excused if he shares the Dauphin's impercipience, for the speaker does not descend to particulars. His enigmatic remark has been taken to mean that by mixing with the common people the Prince acquired a first-hand knowledge of the humbler subjects whom he would command at Agincourt; but the astute politician Bolingbroke sees his son's disregard of royal protocol with misgiving. By making himself 'common-hackneyed in the eyes of men' Hal repeats Richard's mistake, weakening his appeal as a public figure and throwing away political advantage. In exposing himself to the rough-and-tumble of common life the Prince debases the royal standard by submitting it to indignity, and so continues the process initiated by the usurper. If the descent to Eastcheap is seen as a move of enlightened liberalism this significant point is lost. In *Henry V* it evidently suits Shakespeare's purposes to imply that Hal's seemingly irresponsible adventures answered some graver purpose, but the Prince of *Henry IV* appears deliberately to cheapen himself by associating with serving-men and tapsters. He tells Poins,

> I am sworn brother to a leash of drawers, and can call them all by their christen names, as Tom, Dick, and Francis . . . I am so good a proficient in one quarter of an hour that I can drink with any tinker in his own language during my life.
> Pt. 1, ii. 4. 6–19

The tone is obviously ironic. 'Thou hast lost much honour,' Hal concludes with self-depreciating sarcasm, 'that thou wert not with me in this action.' That he does not enjoy the idle futility to which he has condemned himself, or draw any profit from his ignoble schooling, is admitted on one of the few occasions when exasperation gets the better of him:

> Thus we play the fools with the time, and the spirits of the
> wise sit in the clouds and mock us.
>
> Pt. 2, ii. 2. 134f.

The sheer inanity of the episode with Francis, detained by the Prince with huge promises in one room while Poins calls for him in another, invites this disgusted self-reproach. Hal is wasting time fruitlessly, and the discovery that Eastcheap provided an important part of his education is not to be made in this play. Any such discovery is ruled out in advance when the Prince remarks during his opening soliloquy,

> If all the year were playing holidays,
> To sport would be as tedious as to work.
>
> Pt. 1, i. 2. 199f.

The empty existence which the Prince shares with Falstaff serves no constructive purpose. It involves forcing a tedious and wantonly trivial way of life upon a young man whose tastes are entirely serious and responsible, denying him the absorbing occupation which his temperament demands, and compelling him to dissipate his energies upon an endless, exasperating holiday from the crucial affairs about him. The indignity is self–imposed, but the obvious frustration of Hal's serious moral impulse in the frivolous life to which he is committed must rule out any later suggestion that Eastcheap provided valuable experience.

The task of understanding Hal's behaviour is made

more difficult by ambiguities in the plan which he announces in the soliloquy at the end of his first scene. The promise of a reformation which will 'falsify men's hopes' probably does not refer to the legendary change of character at Hal's accession and the heartless rejection of Falstaff. The undertaking is fulfilled at the end of Part 1, when at the battle of Shrewsbury the Prince throws off the disguise of dissolute habits which he has deliberately adopted, and proves his true mettle by overthrowing the rebel Hotspur. The phrase 'falsify men's hopes' is likely to mislead a modern reader, who will see an allusion to Falstaff's expectation of high office under the new king, and not to Hal's disproving of the common judgement of his character. Since the Prince unaccountably returns to his old companions after disclosing his noble character at Shrewsbury, he can enact a similar reformation at the end of Part 2, to which the promise of 'redeeming time when men think least I will' applies a second time. In neither context is Hal to be understood as resolving to drop Falstaff at the most opportune moment for himself. His purpose, indicated in the line

> By how much better than my word I am,
>> Ibid., 205

is to turn a bad reputation to good account; and his intention to 'pay the debt I never promised' hints at a possibly deliberate contrast with Bolingbroke's defrauding and deceit.

This affirmation of plain-dealing is repeated when Hal identifies himself to Douglas at Shrewsbury:

> It is the Prince of Wales that threatens thee,
> Who never promiseth but he means to pay.
>> Pt. 1, v. 4. 41f.

Nothing in the dialogue leading up to this comment invites Hal's remark, but the Prince has just interrupted the combat between the Douglas and Bolingbroke, and is offering himself as challenger and substitute for his father. It would be difficult to resist the implications of the remark, which invites the Douglas to pursue his quarrel with a man who will not default on his personal debts. To say whether Shakespeare intends the Prince to appear conscious and resentful of his father's cheating of his creditors is not possible; but it is clear enough that a direct contrast is being drawn between the two figures. In many important respects Hal presents, as here, an antithesis to Bolingbroke so pointed that his dramatic character seems largely determined by the terms of this inverted relationship. If Falstaff is comic shadow to Bolingbroke, the Prince is his reverse image, duplicating his father's habits in the opposite moral sense, by presenting virtue in the guise of vice. Where Hal's behaviour is not psychologically accountable we may look for its explanation in the imaginative design which obliges him to act as though in deliberate contrast to Bolingbroke, taking a path which tacitly dissociates him from all that his father represents.

The soliloquy, 'I know you all', does more than share the secret of Hal's imposture with the audience. It reveals the biting moral awareness which makes him contemptuous of the character in which he has chosen to disguise his fixed regard for the standards which his father has brought into disrepute. A noble and virtuous young man deliberately masquerading as a dissolute prodigal, Hal is not likely to overlook the deep moral blemishes in his father which he attacks so viciously in Falstaff, who reproduces them in comic form; nor not to have noticed the moral hypocrisy of Bolingbroke's assumption of right. But as the King's subject and heir, Hal is denied all means of expressing his contempt for the dishonourable shifts by which Bolingbroke has maintained his stolen power. By showing such disaffected feeling he would be following the example of Bolingbroke's disloyal behaviour towards his king, and in effect siding with the rebels who now challenge Bolingbroke's fitness to rule. Consequently he can neither support nor oppose his father, and must adopt a third course which places him outside the political conflict, apparently too irresponsible to feel concern for its outcome or his personal reputation. As though taking his lead from the King, who hides his dishonourable record behind a front of kingly authority, the Prince masks his nobility and respect for law by putting on the appearance of contempt for order and justice, so inverting the moral paradox presented by his father.

The character of misrule which he assumes should identify him as Bolingbroke's son, but the King is too deeply absorbed in his role of sanctified monarch to acknowledge the family likeness. Still more ironically, he recognises the counterpart of his younger self in the rebel Hotspur, whom he mistakenly describes as 'the theme of honour's tongue,' and wishes that he might exchange sons with Northumberland:

> O that it could be proved
> That some night-tripping fairy had exchanged
> In cradle-clothes our children where they lay,
> And called mine Percy, his Plantagenet!
>
> Pt. 1, i. 1. 85–88

During the interview for which Hal has practised an answer with Falstaff, Bolingbroke speaks as though the

Prince were bringing disgrace upon a family which hitherto had been untouched by scandal. 'Yet let me wonder, Harry,' he exclaims,

> At thy affections, which do hold a wing
> Quite from the flight of all thy ancestors.
> Pt. 1, iii. 2. 30f.

This may be true, but in a sense other than Bolingbroke intends. To outward appearances Hal's behaviour brands him as a rightful son of the traitor and perjurer who returned illegally from banishment, hypocritically swearing to his limited purposes, and who then deposed the lawful king and cheated his own accomplices. It is Bolingbroke, not his son, who has broken away from ancestral traditions. When he comments that Hal is 'for all the world' like the royal prodigal, Bolingbroke means that he is being as foolish and improvident as Richard before his fall; but his remark admits a second construction, more favourable to the Prince. Although he chooses to conceal his personal nature, Hal is not, like his father, a false thief but a true man who is both loyal and respectful towards the law. His counterpart Hotspur, in whom the King recognises his younger self, is intent upon stealing the crown as Bolingbroke did; and is also trying to disinherit the heir who, in respect of his personal honesty, deserves to be recognised as a true prince and Richard's rightful successor.

Because moral blindness prevents Bolingbroke from seeing himself in his apparently dissolute son, Hal's parentage is called into question. The uncertainty is taken up by Falstaff, who develops the theme comically during his royal performance in the tavern, and so echoes the doubts raised by Bolingbroke several scenes earlier:

138

That thou art my son I have partly thy mother's word, partly my own opinion, but chiefly a villainous trick of thine eye, and a foolish hanging of thy nether lip, that doth warrant me.

Pt. 1, ii. 4. 397–400

A heavily obvious pun in an earlier scene, where Falstaff talks about its being 'here apparent that thou art heir-apparent', touches on the same theme; and when Hal repudiates the suggestion that he should join in a robbery, Falstaff makes the issue a test of the Prince's legitimacy:

Thou cam'st not of the blood royal, if thou darest not stand for ten shillings.

Pt. 1, i. 2. 136f.

Here the joke has a satirical edge, for if Hal can prove his credentials by taking part in a highway robbery, that is because he has a master-thief as father; but the challenge helps to keep alive the question of Hal's parentage. The moral paradox argued by Falstaff, that 'the true prince may, for recreation sake, prove a false thief', involves the same issue and links princely authenticity with criminal habits, though Falstaff's proposal is impudently ambiguous. Beneath the simple meaning 'show himself to be a rascally cutpurse', his statement conceals a suggestion that Hal intends to expose, through his own seeming disrespect for law, the hidden falseness of the royal thief. Falstaff is unconsciously revealing part of the purpose of Hal's playing holidays.

The questioning of his identity concerns Hal through the suggestion that not he but Hotspur is the genuine heir-apparent; an idea which even Bolingbroke helps to encourage. Ignoring the historical fact that Hotspur was Hal's senior by twenty-three years,[1] Shakespeare presents

---

[1] At the Battle of Shrewsbury in 1403 Hotspur was thirty-nine, the Prince sixteen.

them as young men of the same age, whose political hostility is sharpened by a personal antagonism which finds expression on both sides in ridicule. Hotspur's disparaging reference to 'that same sword and buckler Prince of Wales' whom he considers poisoning with a pot of ale is repaid with interest in Hal's sardonic description of his rival, who nonchalantly 'kills me some six or seven dozen of Scots at a breakfast.' They do not meet before their encounter at Shrewsbury, and nothing accounts for their mutual animosity; but both accept the assertion made by Hal before they fight:

> Two stars keep not their motion in one sphere,
> Nor can one England brook a double reign
> Of Harry Percy and the Prince of Wales.
> Pt. 1, v. 4. 64–66

Hal does not merely suggest that there is insufficient room for them both in the kingdom, but that Hotspur and he are bent upon filling a single role, and that one of them must be eliminated. The phrase, 'a double reign', carries its familiar suggestions of equivocal being, explained here by the physical similarity of the two young men who are rivals both for the succession and for the identity of authentic prince. Bolingbroke, who recognises that Hotspur enjoys 'no right, nor colour like to right', argues that none the less his energy and noble spirit give him a stronger claim to the throne than the Prince:

> He hath more worthy interest to the state
> Than thou the shadow of succession.
> Pt. 1, iii. 2. 98f.

The remark is a direct challenge to Hal to prove his authenticity, and a partial explanation of the instinctive dislike which the Prince shows towards Hotspur. By standing out against the chorus of praise to which even his father subscribes, the Prince invites an assumption that he is envious of Hotspur, who usurps the place left vacant by Hal as the natural leader of chivalrous youth, and attracts general admiration by his valour and dash. It is not immediately clear why Hal, seconded by Falstaff, should wish to disparage Hotspur's reputation and to throw doubt upon the authenticity of his exalted code of honour. While the Prince squanders time and good name pursuing trivial pleasures—devising practical jokes, picking Falstaff's pocket, acting interludes in a tavern—Hotspur proves his energy and daring ambition by organising an attack upon the master-thief who has led him into dishonour. His dynamism and sense of purpose offer an astringent contrast to the vapid amusements to which the Prince commits himself. His rebuke to Lady Hotspur, 'Away, you trifler', shows how little he is disposed to spend vital moments upon what he considers the irrelevancies of affection. 'I care not for thee, Kate,' he tells her half-seriously;

> This is no world
> To play with mammets and to tilt with lips.
> Pt. i, ii. 3. 92f.

But his manly sternness is self-conscious and harsh; the attitude of a young man newly entered upon his adult inheritance, and aggressively intent upon displaying a masculine energy of outlook. Recognising that through their past association with Bolingbroke he and his colleagues live 'scandalised and foully spoken of', Hotspur throws himself into a reckless attempt to redeem his good name and to release the kingdom from the dishonour of being ruled by an impudent cut-throat and thief. To this further extent he and the Prince are in agreement, the

descent to Eastcheap representing a silent protest against
the same debasing of noble standards, which Hal cannot
actively oppose. But Hotspur's declaration of purpose,

> To pluck bright honour from the pale-faced moon,
> Or dive into the bottom of the deep,
> Where fathom-line could never touch the ground,
> And pluck up drowned honour by the locks,
>
> Pt. 1, i. 3. 200-3

with its contradictory extremes of leaping and diving,
suggests a new indignity done to honour rather than
restoring her lost prestige; and his ambition of claiming
the entire credit for this salvage operation 'without
corrival' shows how deeply Hotspur's idealism is con-
taminated by self–interest. The undeclared motive of his
headstrong attack upon Bolingbroke is disclosed when he
promises himself, 'That roan shall be my throne.' One
counterfeit is to be evicted by another who hardly troubles
to disguise the illegality of his proceeding when he tells
his wife,

> We must have bloody noses and cracked crowns,
> And pass them current too.
>
> Pt. 1, ii. 3. 94f.

The quibble on broken heads includes the idea of putting
defective coins into circulation as legal tender, and of
repeating the imposture initiated by Bolingbroke, the
uneasy possessor of a figuratively cracked crown. Hotspur's intention increases the irony of Bolingbroke's self-
identification with the rebel leader, who seems to have
modelled himself upon the man who in his time had 'cried
out upon abuses' as Hotspur is doing, to conceal an
unscrupulous private ambition. His political purpose
accounts more completely for the seemingly gratuitous

insults which Hotspur attracts from the Prince. The rival who is seeking to dispossess the rightful heir to Boling-broke's crown will, if he succeeds, frustrate Hal's secret intention of restoring the standards of truth and justice outraged by his father. The bedraggled honour which Hotspur offers to pull up by the locks is as spurious as Bolingbroke's sovereignty, though only the Prince seems awake to the imposture.

Bolingbroke, Hotspur and the Prince have more in common than the name Harry, which helps to suggest an obscure relationship between all three. Each has adopted a moral disguise, the two impostors passing themselves off as authentic, and the true prince deliberately bringing his genuineness into doubt. Bolingbroke grudgingly acknow-ledges his heir, but envies Northumberland his Harry, and wishes their sons might be exchanged; not appreciat-ing that the traitor Harry Hotspur might fittingly regard him as father of his lawless enterprise, and that Hal is indeed a stranger to him except in blood. Their likeness of moral character makes it appropriate that the King should wish to recognise Hotspur as heir, and that Hotspur should act the part of prodigal son to this father-figure; but Hal has imperative reasons for insisting upon his legitimacy, and for offering positive proof of the identity which Hotspur is trying to steal from him. 'I will redeem all this on Percy's head,' he promises Boling-broke;

> And in the closing of some glorious day
> Be bold to tell you that I am your son,
> When I will wear a garment all of blood,
> And stain my favours in a bloody mask,
> Which, washed away, shall scour my shame with it.
> Pt. i, iii. 2. 133–7

143

The images of blood and cleansing carry weighted implications for Bolingbroke, who unlike his son will not be washed clean of the shameful taint of Richard's murder. The Prince will feel able to disclose himself openly only when he has symbolically associated himself with this crime, by appearing masked in blood, and has then washed off the stain of inherited guilt by killing the pretender in whom Bolingbroke's vices are renewed. In the defeat which is to demonstrate Hotspur's spurious-ness the moral tables will be turned upon him, so that while Hal proves himself the rightful prince, Hotspur will appear in his true character, hitherto assumed by Hal:

> I shall make this northern youth exchange
> His glorious deeds for my indignities . . .
> And I will call him to so strict account
> That he shall render every glory up.
>
> Ibid., 145–50

At Shrewsbury the dispute is settled by Hal's victory over the plausible double who has usurped his place hitherto. Once discredited by force of arms, Hotspur's imposture reveals itself immediately in the collapsing of his heroic figure. Hal's comment over his enemy's body,

> Ill-weaved ambition, how much art thou shrunk!
>
> Pt. 1, v. 4. 87

suggests that his sword has punctured an inflated dummy whose empty shell now proves the impudence of Hot-spur's impersonation. Falstaff completes the exposure by dishonouring Hotspur's body with a wound closely akin to the ritual mutilation of condemned traitors, and takes the corpse on his back—the early texts are explicit on this point—in the fashion of a Morality devil bearing off one of the damned.[1]

Hal's descent to the murky world of the taverns does not prepare him for kingship. It represents the adoption of a moral attitude exactly opposite to the position taken up by Bolingbroke and Hotspur in common, a mask of dishonour assumed as though in protest against the spurious nobility of both. The audience is invited to recognise the Prince as the moral antithesis of Bolingbroke, and to find assurance in Hal's behaviour that the next king will reverse all the practices by which Bolingbroke has corrupted law and truth. The killing of Hotspur, an image of the prince whom Bolingbroke wishes his son to be, is an earnest of Hal's ultimate intention. The purpose which he discloses at his accession admits more than his own past wildness. 'The tide of blood in me,' he tells the Lord Chief Justice,

> Hath proudly flowed in vanity till now;
> Now doth it turn and ebb back to the sea,
> Where it shall mingle with the state of floods,
> And flow henceforth in formal majesty.
>
> Pt. 2, v. 2. 130–3

The tide withdrawing from inland creeks to the open sea represents the Prince who has abandoned Eastcheap for ever, but much more the final dissociation of the blood-royal from the dishonours which Bolingbroke rather than Hal has brought upon it. Although Hal's moral reformation involves some calculated pretence, it is not simply hypocritical. The change of character which he appears to undergo is a true index of the transformation worked

---

[1] The posture of the victim, who hangs head downwards along the devil's back, his knees flexed over the devil's shoulders, appears frequently in medieval conography.

upon the king's office and person as Hal restores dignity
to both. By concealing his nobility until the moment of his
accession, he is able to show in himself how completely
sovereignty is to renounce its long association with crime.
A prince who had not disguised his respect for law would
be incapable of making this deeply symbolic gesture,
whose purpose is not to illuminate Hal's character but to
round off the imaginative design of the play in a strong
dramatic image.

Immediately before this closing episode of the play Hal
has made an almost explicit repudiation of Bolingbroke's
unprincipled standards when he takes the crown from his
father's bedside. To Bolingbroke, this seeming theft is
the final proof of his son's contempt for legal right and
ordered ritual: to the audience, another variation on the
political theme which has occupied Shakespeare throughout the history-plays. Outward appearances suggest that
Hal is successor to a long line of political adventurers
intoxicated by the lure of the crown, as Bolingbroke
himself had been. Having snatched the prize 'with
boisterous hand', the King has lived to regret his impulsiveness, and is about to die exhausted by the prolonged
strain of resisting attacks upon his unstable authority.
His warning to Hal,

> O foolish youth!
> Thou seek'st the greatness that will overwhelm thee:
>> Pt. 2, iv. 5. 96f.

derives from his own disillusioning experience, and would
be applied justly to a son following his own mistaken
example. But Bolingbroke does not appreciate Hal's
motives in taking the crown. The moralising comment by
which he rebukes the covetousness he wrongly attributes
to the Prince,

How quickly nature falls into revolt
When gold becomes her object!
Ibid., 65f.

has a fitting application to his own experience. He
shows the same imperceptiveness as he continues his
reflections, commiserating with the 'foolish, over-careful
fathers' who, to assure their heirs a fortune,

Have broke their sleep with thoughts,
Their brains with care, their bones with industry;
For this they have engrossed and piled up
The cankered heaps of strange-achieved gold.
Ibid., 68–71

The epithet 'strange-achieved' acts as clue to the ironic
sense of Bolingbroke's lament over the wealth squandered
by a prodigal son. The gold which has cost him much
unremitting effort and anxiety is the crown, 'strange-
achieved' in the wrongful means by which he gained it.
He must now, Bolingbroke believes, suffer the characteristic fate of the scraping father whose laboriously achieved
fortune is dissipated by a son's wild extravagance. In fact
Bolingbroke is a moral bankrupt who can bequeath only
dishonour to his son, and the bitter taste left in a mouth
once 'packed with honey'[1] comes from the disillusioning
of his political hopes, not from Hal's supposed wish to
seize the crown before the inheritance is due. The Prince
takes the crown from the bedside soberly aware of its
destructive power—'Thou best of gold art worst of gold'—
and puts it on his head

To try with it, as with an enemy
That had before my face murdered my father,
The quarrel of a true inheritor.
Ibid., 166–8

[1] The passage is characteristic of Shakespeare in linking images of
honey and theft.

147

Unlike the unlawful claimants of the earlier Histories, on whom the crown acts like a madness, the Prince is immune to the promise of personal magnificence which it has held out to so many reckless victims. 'If any rebel or vain spirit of mine,' he tells Bolingbroke,

> Did with the least affection of a welcome
> Give entertainment to the might of it,
> Let God for ever keep it from my head.
>
> Ibid., 172–4

As at Gad's Hill, the stolen property is returned; and the long sequence of prodigal sons is interrupted by the heir who instead of killing his rich father out of haste for his inheritance, attacks the force which has destroyed him. This winding-up of imagery which has persisted from *Richard II* suggests that the conclusion of *Henry IV* represents the culmination of a particular imaginative thread, and the resolution of an issue which had evaded Shakespeare hitherto. After the repeated affirmations of this scene that the Prince will take the crown by due right of succession, and as undisputed heir,[1] at his next appearance the play takes on an assurance of tone which seems only partly explained by the royal dignity which Hal has acquired. In the young king's unforced assumption of majesty, Shakespeare seems to convey a sense of his own creative achievement as he brings the complex imaginative issues of his first great play to a stabilised close.

Hal's demonstration of respect for the legal possession of the crown is followed by a second mark of his determination to restore the force and authority of law. His first act as king is to reinvest the Lord Chief Justice with the

[1] See Pt. 2, iv. 5. 168, 187f., 199–201, 221f.

insignia of the office which he has exercised fearlessly, even to the extent of committing the Prince to prison for striking him. Challenged on this point and expecting no reprieve, the Lord Chief Justice defends the action which he had taken on behalf of the father whom he represented. 'Be you contented, wearing now the garland,' he asks the new king,

> To have a son set your decrees at naught?
> To pluck down Justice from your aweful bench;
> To trip the course of law, and blunt the sword
> That guards the peace and safety of your person?
> Nay more, to spurn at your most royal image,
> And mock your workings in a second body?
>
> Pt. 2, v. 2. 85–90

His questions are more pertinent than the speaker realises. Although it is the riotous prince who, it seems, has made a mock of established law, the legal processes to which the Lord Chief Justice refers have been much more gravely damaged by Bolingbroke. He, and not Hal, has plucked down Justice from her bench and brought disrepute upon the ordered purposes which safeguard the king's own position. The impostor who would ridicule the figure of majesty by aping its functions 'in a second body' is not the true prince, who is about to honour the institution of justice, but the father who he now symbolically rejects. Hal's answer to the Lord Chief Justice,

> You are right Justice, and you weigh this well;
> Therefore still bear the balance and the sword
>
> Ibid., 102f.

suggests that by reaffirming his readiness to commit even a royal offender to prison, this principal officer of state has passed a crucial test. In a kingdom where until recently the sovereign has brought the law into disrepute this scrutiny has special point. The indignation which the Lord Chief Justice feels towards the duplicating of supreme authority involves a silent repudiation of Bolingbroke, and of the equivocal standards from which the Prince has broken away much earlier. This severance, more from his tarnished ancestry than from his disreputable past, becomes absolute when the young king disowns the dissolute figure who has been 'the tutor and the feeder' of lawlessness, and adopts as father the representative of settled order and equity. 'Here is my hand,' he tells the Lord Chief Justice, newly appointed to the post which Falstaff has promised himself;

> You shall be as a father to my youth,
> My voice shall sound as you do prompt mine ear,
> And I will stoop and humble my intents
> To your well-practised wise directions.
>
> Ibid., 118–21

This reinstating of justice after the confusions of Bolingbroke's imposture restores the positive standards which the old king's falseness has thrown into question. By presenting his actual nobility as dishonour, Hal has made himself a stranger to the inverted moral values upheld by Bolingbroke, and shown his critical discrimination between the substance and form of truth; while the King, through habitual counterfeiting, has lost this power of distinguishing between the false and the authentic. The new king now brings his discrimination to bear upon the ambiguous appearances which have checked and harassed the process of law during the reign of a usurper, and chooses without hesitation between the real and the spurious figures of justice which claim the office. In making this disclosure of his true self, Hal also restores the image of sovereignty defaced by his father, whose dissimulating

of royalty set an example for doubling and equivocation throughout his kingdom. With the passing of old
Double and the public rejection of the father-figure in
whom Bolingbroke's vices are impudently parodied, the
moral inversions of the reign are brought to an end. The
prodigal father is succeeded by a just son; and the royal
estate is inherited by an heir whose personal truth, in
its various senses, is made imaginatively equivalent with
an unchallengeable right to the name of king.

IV. THE REBELS

The ironies which have their principal focus in Bolingbroke extend to all the major figures and events of the
play. In particular, they act upon the rebels, whose
kindred nature with Bolingbroke is evident in their
attempts to emulate his seizing of power. Once possessed
of the crown, Bolingbroke chooses to forget that he was
ever a rebel; and either in his own person or through a
spokesman he denounces the associates who are now
following his lawless example by attempting to overthrow their king. The terms of his denunciation, we have
already noticed, apply to himself with equal force;
unconsciously admitting his moral imposture and illegality
of proceeding. 'If that rebellion came like itself,' Westmoreland observes to the Archbishop and his supporters,

> In his true, native and most proper shape,
> You, reverend father, and these noble lords
> Had not been here, to dress the ugly form
> Of base and bloody insurrection
> With your fair honours.
>
> Pt. 2, iv. 1. 37–41

Bolingbroke has been their example in this disguising of
shameful purposes. If Westmoreland's remark has any

moral justice, it finds a more appropriate target in the 'fair honours' which mask Bolingbroke's guilt than in the half-hearted claim of the northern rebels to personify right. But beside being without his personal authority, Bolingbroke's enemies lack his politician's talent for passing off private ambition as disinterested concern for the public good, and the meanness of their intentions is never well concealed. The idea of exacting punishment for the murder of Richard is soon abandoned for the more attractive prospect of winning a share in a stolen kingdom, though at Shrewsbury the rebels claim only to be acting in self-defence. The spokesman of the northern rebels seems to admit the desperateness of their course by telling Westmoreland, 'We are all diseased'; but then suggests that their rising is designed only as a terrifying show of arms, to act as a cathartic upon

> obstructions which begin to stop
> Our very veins of life.
>
> Ibid., 65f.

This uncertainty of purpose in the rebels, and the absence of any persuasive moral argument to strengthen their public cause, constitute a political weakness which Bolingbroke had never allowed himself. In both *Richard II* and *Henry IV* he seems to have justice on his side if not the strict approval of law, and he speaks as though sincerely concerned for the well-being of the kingdom whose moral health he destroys. The seeming genuineness of this concern runs deep enough for Bolingbroke himself to be convinced of his good intentions, and incapable of recognising himself as a rebel. His old confederates, much more thinly disguised as public benefactors and more blatantly intent upon enriching themselves, reveal the character from which Bolingbroke attempts, never quite successfully, to dissociate himself. Beneath the regalia and majestic manner of a king his effrontery is greater, if less obvious, than theirs, and his fundamental purpose no different. Their presence, and their efforts to attract support to a morally worthless cause, provide a recurrent reminder of the dishonourable background which Bolingbroke seems to have thrust out of mind.

The character which the rebels share with Bolingbroke is not limited to their profession of disinterested purpose. Like him, they become victims of an enigmatic design working through political events, whose course frustrates their private intentions after seeming initially to promise success. This disappointing of early hopes, usually by an ironic reversal of fortune in the moment of achievement, figures in *Henry IV* as a motif persistent enough to be taken as a major concept of the play. If *Henry IV* offers a view of history, the ironies of man's inability to foresee the course of political events figure prominently in it. Towards the end of his unquiet reign, Bolingbroke can appreciate though still not forestall the ironic disclosures brought by the working of time. His cry to Warwick,

> O God! that one might read the book of fate,
> And see the revolution of the times
>
> Pt. 2, iii. 1. 45f.

voices the despair of a man outwitted by the deviousness of a force either disregarded or mistaken for an ally:

> The happiest youth, viewing his progress through,
> What perils passed, what crosses to ensue,
> Would shut the book, and sit him down and die.
>
> Ibid., 54–56

Of the two challenges mounted against Bolingbroke by

the rebels, the first ends disastrously through lack of foresight and cold-headed planning, the second despite the seasoned judgement and calculation which direct its progress up to the moment of confrontation. The northern rebels are wide awake to the likelihood of unexpected checks to their carefully shaped project; but their realistic caution deserts them when they reach the verge of success, and they are overwhelmed as completely as the impulsive Hotspur, whose headstrong spirit dominates the earlier attempt. A gambler too obstinate and self-confident to weigh the hazards of failure—'If he fall in, good night!'—and too impatient for action to respect strategical issues, Hotspur urges the rebellion forward faster than it can gather its full weight, and arrives at Shrewsbury with only half the forces which he had counted upon. His contempt for the friend who declines his invitation to join the conspiracy shows Hotspur's naïvety both in the planning of a military operation and in the reckoning of its likely development. Nettled by the criticism of his wary correspondent, who describes the enterprise as too dangerous,

> the friends you have named uncertain, the time itself unsorted, and your whole plot too light for the counterpoise of so great an opposition
>
> Pt. 1, ii. 3. 12–14

Hotspur defends the rebels' plan with the simple credulity of a man incapable of questioning his own assumptions:

> By the lord, our plot is good plot as ever was laid, our friends true and constant: a good plot, good friends, and full of expectation: an excellent plot, very good friends.
>
> Ibid., 16–19

When he runs over the outline of their plan Hotspur is

not restoring a shaken confidence, but expressing uncritical amazement that it should not impress an outsider
as it does himself:

> Is there not my father, my uncle, and myself; Lord Edmund
> Mortimer, my lord of York, and Owen Glendower? Is there
> not besides the Douglas? Have I not all their letters to meet
> me in arms by the ninth of the next month, and are they not
> some of them set forward already?
>
> Ibid., 23–29

His recapitulation reveals what the plot amounts to on
paper, but not what it may produce in the field. When
news of the uprising reaches Bolingbroke it should,
Falstaff suggests pleasantly, turn his beard white with
fear; and Blunt does not try to depreciate the gravity of
the threat. 'A mighty and a fearful head they are,' he tells
the King,

> If promises be kept on every hand.
>
> Pt. 1, iii. 2. 168

Bolingbroke should know how conveniently promises are
sometimes forgotten, but he does not count upon defec-
tions to reduce the rebels' numbers. His enemies, on the
other hand, make no allowance for unforeseen checks and
disappointments. The conspiracy is translated into action
with a speed that does not permit second thoughts, and
with no attempt to anticipate the kind of strategical set-
back which is to lame its whole endeavour. Worcester
alone seems to possess the calculating mind which could
produce a more cautious reckoning; but knowing himself
beyond hope of Bolingbroke's pardon he supports
Hotspur's recklessness, a penniless gambler making his
last throw. The second conspiracy-scene opens with an
optimistic review of the rebels' prospects by Mortimer:

155

These promises are fair, the parties sure,
And our induction full of prosperous hope:

Pt. 1, iii. 1. 1f.

after which the conspirators set about determining how
Bolingbroke's kingdom is to be shared between them.
The outcome proves how ironically loaded are the terms
'promise', 'sure', and 'hope' in this play. The rebels of
Part 1 have no realistic accomplice to warn them, as
Bardolph will warn his fellow-conspirators in the northern
rebellion, that

> In a theme so bloody-faced as this,
> Conjecture, expectation, and surmise
> Of aids incertain should not be admitted.

Pt. 2, i. 3. 22–24

The northern rebels can profit from the example of
Hotspur's ruinous failure, where a leader 'lined himself
with hope, eating the air on promise of supply', and
in the trial of strength found himself supported by a
phantom army, 'but the shadows and the shows of men.'
In Part 2 Bardolph speaks as though there had been some
judicious weighing of circumstances. 'You cast th'event
of war,' he reminds Northumberland,

> And summed the account of chance, before you said
> 'Let us make head.'

Pt. 2, i. 1. 167f.

Nothing is heard of this in Part 1. Bardolph recalls the
spirit of the Percies' rebellion more exactly when he
remarks that the rebels acknowledged an element of sheer
risk in their undertaking, but accepted the gamble in the
interest of the prize at stake. 'We ventured on such
dangerous seas,' he admits,

That if we wrought out life 'twas ten to one;
And yet we ventured, for the gain proposed
Choked the respect of likely peril feared.
                              Ibid., 182–4

The speaker tactfully refrains from observing that one of
the major hazards has been Northumberland's sliding
resolution, which is about to display itself for a second
time. By deciding not to commit himself to the rebels'
cause before the trial of strength at Shrewsbury, Northumberland gives a blow to his friends' expectations which
Hotspur frankly acknowledges as 'a perilous gash, a
very limb lopped off'. But immediately a rush of confidence overwhelms his better judgement, and Hotspur
argues implausibly that to fight the battle without
Northumberland will be a positive advantage, since the
rebels will not then gamble their whole fortune on a
single throw. 'Were it good,' Hotspur demands,

To set the exact wealth of all our states
All at one cast? To set so rich a main
On the nice hazard of one doubtful hour?
                         Pt. i, iv. i. 46–8

His argument ignores the likelihood that if the 'doubtful
hour' at Shrewsbury goes against them, the rebels will
find no second opportunity of challenging Bolingbroke.
Douglas seconds this improvident proposal. The rebels,
he declares, may now boldly put their seriously weakened
forces to the test 'upon hope' of the reserve withheld by
Northumberland. The collapse of such a hope only a few
moments earlier has taught them nothing. Douglas has
sense enough to realise that, besides maiming their
military strength, Northumberland's defection must
check the confidence of their supporters:

This absence of your father's draws a curtain
That shows the ignorant a kind of fear
Before not dreamt of.

Ibid., 73–75

But when Hotspur retorts that the absence of a powerful
ally lends lustre 'and more great opinion'[1] to their enterprise, Douglas drops his objection. If the rebels are
prepared to confront Bolingbroke without Northumberland's support, Hotspur asserts, it must be obvious to
the world at large that their combined strengths will be
irresistible. By what means Northumberland will be
persuaded to throw his military weight against the King
Hotspur does not reveal. This last suggestion characterises the disregard of unwelcome fact and strategical
disadvantage which is to prove suicidal. More unexpected
reverses are to come. Vernon cuts away a little more of the
ground under Hotspur's feet by bringing news that
Glendower cannot gather his forces for another two weeks.
Mortimer too fails to keep his military rendezvous,
though without checking Hotspur's now wildly headstrong impatience to throw his much depleted army
against Bolingbroke. The rush of events before battle
allows Hotspur no time, had he the impulse, to reflect
upon the abject collapse of 'an excellent plot, very good
friends'. Undeterred by the progressive discrediting of
his hopes, he refuses to modify the simple plan of a direct
confrontation with a powerful enemy, and continues to
behave as though he and not Bolingbroke enjoyed the
tactical advantage. At Shrewsbury he wishes to attack
before his badly outnumbered forces have completely
assembled, and when Worcester's cavalry is jaded by its
hurried march. Vernon's objection that

[1] *Opinion* prestige.

> Their pride and mettle is asleep,
> Their courage with hard labour tame and dull,
> That not a horse is half the half himself;
>
> Pt. i, iv. 3. 22–24

has ominous overtones; implying that this depressed and sluggish spirit may extend to the rebel troops, reluctant to fight in a doubtful cause, and now facing a sharply increased prospect of defeat. Vernon expresses astonishment that 'men of such great leading' as Hotspur and Douglas, who seconds this wild proposal, should contemplate so harebrained a plan; but Hotspur sees the presence of an unmolested enemy as a rebuke to his personal honour, and is ready to throw all tactical considerations to the winds. When Vernon and Worcester refuse to pit a tired and half-organised army against superior forces, their council-of-war degenerates into a juvenile quarrel about personal bravery, and the plan for an immediate attack is shelved only because the conspirators are interrupted by Blunt's request for a parley.

Hotspur's defeat follows almost as a matter of course. The setbacks which sap the vitality of his army and drain its initial confidence have been unforeseen in his wild impatience to come to blows with Bolingbroke:

> O let the hours be short,
> Till fields, and blows, and groans applaud our sport!
>
> Pt. i, i. 3. 295f.

The rebellion is launched with the prospect of developing a force which Bolingbroke sees as a massive threat to his unsteady régime, but this mighty opposition never materialises. Hotspur's prospect of success rests upon hopes and promises so persuasive that, when they wilt, he seems not to recognise his impotence as commander of a shadow-army. 'He apprehends a world of figures here,' Worcester remarks of him during the first scene of the conspiracy,

> But not the form of what he should attend.
>
> Ibid., 208

Like other characters of the play, Hotspur mistakes shadow for substance. He never awakes to the actuality of his most potent and ironic enemy: the working of events which follow a course of their own and resist all man's attempts to impress his own purpose upon them.

The second phase of rebellion opens with a severely realistic appreciation of the hazards to be accepted. Unlike their ruined confederates, the Archbishop and his followers are alive to the danger of depending on untested assumptions and buoyant hopes. The crucial question facing the rebels is whether they can count upon raising a force strong enough to challenge Bolingbroke. The Archbishop's three advisers include an optimist, Hastings, who argues that some expectations are positive enough to be counted upon. 'It never yet did hurt,' he maintains against Bardolph's warning that Hotspur was lured to death by empty assurances of support,

> To lay down likelihoods and forms of hope.
>
> Pt. 2, i. 3. 35

Bardolph resists this dangerous argument with some energy. It does harm, he replies, when an enterprise goes forward upon hopes which prove as deceptive as the encouragements of an early spring:

> Yes, if this present quality of war—
> Indeed the instant action, a cause on foot—
> Lives so in hope, as in an early spring

We see th'appearing buds; which to prove fruit
Hope gives not so much warrant, as despair
That frosts will bite them.

Ibid., 36–41

Developing his point, Bardolph insists that before they
commit themselves to so momentous a project—'which is
almost to pluck a kingdom down And set another up'—
they must calculate their means and resources exactly, if
they are not to embark upon an undertaking which they
cannot carry through. Hastings admits that their hopes
of support may come to nothing, but believes that the
rebels are strong enough to declare themselves without
the reinforcement which he expects to materialise.
Bolingbroke has to guard himself against possible attacks
from three different quarters, Hastings continues, and
cannot concentrate his armed strength against a rebellion
in the north. The Archbishop concurs:

That he should draw his several strengths together
And come against us in full puissance,
Need not be dreaded.

Ibid., 76–78

Events prove him right, and support the decision to go
forward in the acceptance of a reasonable risk. Not looking
beyond the army of twenty-five thousand men which they
themselves can muster, the rebels have made an accurate
prediction of the way events are likely to develop, refusing
to entertain hopes of lucky windfalls. In particular, and in
this respect pointedly unlike Hotspur, they have recognised the complete unreliability of Northumberland, and
have put him firmly out of their calculations. With his
support, the rebel forces would be more than a match for
Bolingbroke; but Hotspur's venture foundered on just
this mistaken dependence, and the northern rebels will

not repeat his error. The good sense of their wariness appears later, when although insisting that his personal honour 'is at pawn' through his engagement to the rebels, Northumberland gives way ignominiously to the advice of his womenfolk, and retires to Scotland to await the outcome of the conflict. At the news of this second defection, Mowbray observes that their hopes of vital support 'touch ground and dash themselves to pieces'; but the rebels have reckoned themselves strong enough without this uncertain reinforcement, and have not fatally exposed themselves.

When the armies confront each other, the rebels see their predictions substantially confirmed. Bolingbroke has been unable to detach a force great enough to outnumber the rebels, and the Archbishop enjoys a parity of strength denied to Hotspur at Shrewsbury. He has also a more confident body of supporters, and faces an enemy weary of political conflict, whose energy 'like to a fangless lion' no longer seems dangerous. The Archbishop is not entirely disposed to welcome the changed conditions which favour their cause, seeing the shift of popular support from Bolingbroke to themselves as a characteristic mark of fickleness in the common people:

> An habitation giddy and unsure
> Hath he that buildeth on the vulgar heart.
> Ibid., 89f.

His remark awakes an echo of Bardolph's caution earlier in the scene, that those who plan political overthrow must first 'consent upon a sure foundation'. The warning is obliquely ratified in the Archbishop's cry of disgust at the hypocrisy of Bolingbroke's pretences, 'What trust is in these times?' This insecurity extends further than the

Archbishop yet realises. The rebels have refused to count upon good luck or to entertain hopes which might encourage a false sense of their military strength. Laying their plans circumspectly, they reach the point which they had foreseen, where they meet a royal army no greater than their own and inferior in morale. At this point, where a determined thrust might have toppled Bolingbroke, the rebels throw in their hand upon the most specious of assurances, and are themselves crushed effortlessly.

The promises which they accept so trustfully from Prince John are as deceptive as the intimations described by the Archbishop as he pledges his enemies:

> Against ill chances men are ever merry,
> But heaviness foreruns the good event.
>
> iv. 2 81f.

Mowbray alone stands out against the agreement with Prince John, objecting that Bolingbroke will not easily forget their rebellion; but he is overruled by his confederates, who promise themselves a more favourable future. Hastings, who threatens the Prince with a succession of rebellions should their own miscarry, is dismissed scornfully as

> much too shallow
> To sound the bottom of the after-times.
>
> Ibid., 5of.

The truth of the criticism soon appears. Confident in their strength and in Bolingbroke's spiritual exhaustion, the rebels snatch eagerly at the offer of a negotiated settlement, and dismiss their troops with no other security than Prince John's bare assurance. It is again only the mistrustful Mowbray who resists the hypocritical promise, becoming 'on the sudden something ill' when he has allowed his confederates to silence his misgivings. The jocularity of the Archbishop's remark, intended to dispel this fear, indicates how rapidly he has lost touch with the dangerous realities of the situation. His happy admission, 'Believe me, I am passing light in spirit', makes him seem already tipsy with thoughtless exuberance as he swallows Prince John's wine and empty promises with the same credulity. Mowbray sourly points out the corollary to the Archbishop's remark,

> So much the worse, if your own rule be true;
> Ibid., 85

and shows that the man previously alert to the danger of optimistic expectation has lost all sense of caution. The shock of arrest destroys the illusion of security without making the Archbishop aware of his deeper credulity. The outraged question, 'Will you thus break your faith?' proves him deceived not only by Prince John's callous hypocrisy but by the promising appearances which he had taken on trust.

The eclipse of the second rebellion, overwhelmed despite the rebels' attempts to avoid Hotspur's ruinous mistakes, demonstrates the futility of attempting to foresee and forestall the shifts of fortune on which political success depends. In this respect once again the rebels share the experience of the man they are attempting to unseat. Like them, Bolingbroke discovers eventually that he has failed to foresee the major consequences of his political actions, and that the forces he thought to direct have made him their victim. Both he and the rebels realise, too late to make use of their knowledge, that the energies of political ambition are powerless to impose their will upon the

great area of happening which encloses the narrow sector
of their private interests. In Warwick the ageing Bolingbroke possesses a counsellor able to trace out the obscure
design which runs through his experience, yet the
unpredictable outcome of events has an irony for the
King which brings him near to despair. To Bolingbroke,
Northumberland's repeated reversal of allegiance seems
characteristic of the merely whimsical inconstancy of
fortune:

> How chances mock,
> And changes fill the cup of alteration
> With divers liquors.
>
> Pt. 2, iii. 1. 51–53

It is still more incomprehensible to the King that Richard
could foresee Northumberland's disloyalty to Bolingbroke
at a time when Northumberland was the most zealous of
the usurper's supporters—even, as Bolingbroke avers to
Warwick, before he had seriously considered assuming
the crown. His evidently genuine bewilderment at the
fulfilment of Richard's prophecy requires us to credit
Bolingbroke's otherwise implausible claim. The crown has
come into his hands with no active conspiracy on his part;
and Northumberland has turned against the usurper who,
when Richard foretold this betrayal of a second royal
master, had still to make himself king.

There may be some contradiction between Bolingbroke's apparently genuine inability to explain what
brought him to the throne, and Shakespeare's portrayal
of an unscrupulous politician who has taken the crown by
improvising upon advantage. The Bolingbroke of *Richard
II* returns from exile as a political gambler, without
support or assurance of means great enough to overthrow
Richard. If he counts upon his popularity he follows no

definite plan, and achieves success by exploiting weaknesses in Richard which the most optimistic forecast
could not have expected. In this respect the ease of his
almost unresisted sweep to the throne might have surprised him; though the idea of supplanting Richard
begins to impel him as soon as he recognises his gathering
strength. He has the king's favourites executed long
before the question of deposing Richard has been formally
raised; and the opening of the deposition-scene shows
him abrogating other royal prerogatives while Richard is
still king in name and form of law. This is not the behaviour
of a man who had royalty thrust upon him unawares. But
events of *Richard II* cannot be used to corroborate or
dispute assertions made in a later play, where Shakespeare's purposes may have changed; as in this respect it
appears they have. The scene with Warwick shows
Bolingbroke deeply shaken by a long-delayed realisation
that his actions have recoiled upon him, and that the
unstable world of political affairs upon which he has
spent himself has never been under his control. Other
purposes, more powerful and cryptic than his own limited
ambitions, have decided the outcome of private hopes
which the rebels have seen dashed in the same mocking
fashion.

These ironies of expectation form a recurrent motif of
Henry IV: a play in which the Prince alone, a self-isolated
onlooker, cannot be surprised by the cruelly comic
reversal of hopes. Shakespeare might be expressing a
personal view of history through the forms of ironic
disappointment that recur so frequently in the action,
involving king, rebel and potboy in a common collapse of
hopeful designs. More probably, this persistent interest
springs from the imaginative peroccupation with identity

which is pursued less intensively in *Richard II*. As poet, Shakespeare displays an unwearied interest in the true and false natures of things; in duplicity and seeming, and the counterfeiting of reality which is the aim of acting. This interest declares itself in the Sonnets, and is a growing theme of the early plays. In *Henry IV* it becomes a complex major motif, impressed upon the action as well as upon individual character. The design of events proves as deceptive to Falstaff as to the rebels, and finally embraces the King. His usurped reign ends appropriately in the discovery that, after a lifetime of counterfeiting, equivocations greater than he has imposed upon a disturbed kingdom have made him their tragicomic victim.

CHAPTER IV

The True Inheritor

THE play which follows the two parts of *Henry IV* is both a surprise and a disappointment. Whatever qualities of good and bad may be claimed for it, *Henry V* is a work radically unlike any other of Shakespeare's history-plays in general style and structure. Instead of a con-tinuous dramatic development, it offers its audience a disjointed succession of scenes or groups of scenes in chronicle fashion, related not by persistent imaginative themes but by common subject-matter; binding them loosely together through the commentary of a Chorus who presents the play. The activity of this presenter—himself an admission of structural weakness in the play, which should carry itself forward—recurrently diverts the audience's attention from dramatic events to the dramatic illusion in which they are to immerse themselves. The spectators are explicitly reminded that they are in the playhouse, watching a performance which falls abjectly short of its great subject; and asked to help the poet by bringing their own imaginations to bear upon the story and its figures. These appeals and apologies have a deferential charm, and an immediate power, which make the speeches of the Chorus an attractive feature of *Henry V;* but his apologies for the play's shortcomings are as curious as his pleas to the audience to support weak writing by imagining the scene. It is possible that these apologies are not intended very seriously, and that the poet who begins by wishing for a Muse of fire is about to demonstrate a competence in other fields than rhetoric. On the other hand the obvious weakness of the play's dramatic structure might invite some form of apology from a poet whose audience had seen much better craftsmanship in *Henry IV*. The speeches of the Chorus anticipate the kind of criticism which Shakespeare might reasonably have expected, and bring courtesy and frankness to his rescue.

Although this frankness does not extend so far as admitting a lack of imaginative drive, little suggests that Shakespeare was imaginatively committed to the characters and events of *Henry V*, or to whatever view of life it might contain. The presence of the Chorus as interpreter between the action and the audience, and his reminders that they are in the playhouse together, shows a disposition to regard the play as a piece of entertainment in which the spectators are not personally involved. Shakespeare seems to be standing away from the scenes which the Chorus presents; giving his presenter a dramatic immediacy and force not often found in the play itself, and then using his authority to urge the audience to participate imaginatively in dramatic events which have no such compulsion. However persuasively the Chorus paints the scene, it is difficult not to feel a sense of anxiety and strain beneath his repeated promptings to spectators who must devise elaborate scenic effects at the poet's bidding. The persistent imperatives of these speeches—'Piece out our imperfections', 'work, work your thoughts', 'grapple your minds'—suggest a degree of almost muscular effort as the poet struggles to set an unyielding train of ideas in motion. The same impulse is felt several times in the play itself, characteristically in the Archbishop's encouragement to the King to delay no longer:

> Stand for your own; unwind your bloody flag;
> Look back into your mighty ancestors:
> Go, my dread lord, to your great-grandsire's tomb,
> From whom you claim; invoke his warlike spirit.
>
> i. 2. 101–104

Like the English soldiers before Harfleur, Shakespeare seems to be under pressure to summon up spirit for an enterprise which does not itself excite creative enthusiasm. His use of long descriptive speeches to set the physical scene of the play is one of its many surprising features. Nothing of the kind is attempted in *Henry IV*, which like all the earlier Histories concentrates its dramatic attention upon human actions and events, without regard to physical setting. The long set speeches of *Henry V*— those of the Archbishop in i. 2, the King in iv. 1, and of Burgundy in v. 2 are typical[1]—suggest that despite its association with warfare, the character of the play is predominantly static. One may go further than this and assert that an imaginative awareness of inertia, of paralysed immobility, is one of the few realised poetic features of *Henry V*: a point which must be examined more closely later. While it would be absurd to suggest that the play never breaks out of lethargy into vigorous action, *Henry V* is never convincingly moved by the sense of developing events which gives other plays their dramatic life. Shakespeare's historical matter seems intractable, refusing to come properly to life despite his efforts to force its disparate elements to coalesce and move together. The disjointed form of the play reflects his difficulties,

[1] Respectively 63, 55 and 55 lines long.

and the speeches of the Chorus seek pardon for inadequacies which the poet blames, not very plausibly, upon
the magnitude of his subject. The world of *Henry IV*
involved greater creative problems, which Shakespeare
solved without drawing attention to the ambitious scope
of his play.

Because *Henry V* refuses to work by developing its own
dramatic momentum, Shakespeare falls back upon a mode
of direct descriptive writing in place of fully dramatic
dialogue. The scenic background provided by the Chorus,
which gives the play the intermittent character of a
narrative poem, is the most obvious example of this tendency to describe rather than to enact. Description is not
limited to physical setting. Before Act 3 the Chorus
rapidly sketches in the events leading to the attack on
Harfleur, asking the audience to fill in gaps in the story:

> Suppose th'ambassador from the French comes back;
> Tells Harry that the king doth offer him
> Katherine his daughter; and with her, to dowry,
> Some petty and unprofitable dukedoms:
> The offer likes not: and the nimble gunner
> With linstock now the devilish cannon touches.
>
> III. 28–33

The narration hurries over the kind of ambassadorial
exchange that might have been allowed a short scene in
Henry IV, in order to reach the rhetorical high-point of
the King's address to his troops; which, for all its flexing
of muscles, contributes nothing actively dramatic to the
play. Act V begins after a still more perfunctory outlining
of events between the King's return to England and his
second landing in France: an explanation of no dramatic
value, since there is no shift of action from the French
setting of Act IV. The account of this empty interval

given by the Chorus may have suffered textual corruption, but without concealing Shakespeare's use of sketchy narrative to solder episodes of the play crudely together:

> As yet the lamentation of the French
> Invites the King of England's stay at home;
> The emperor's coming in behalf of France,
> To order peace between them; and omit
> All the occurrences, whatever chanc'd,
> Till Harry's back-return again to France.
>
> V. 36–41

Nothing is gained dramatically by separating the events of Act V from the victory at Agincourt; and since Shakespeare's deference to historical fact obliges Fluellen to delay his reckoning with Pistol until the King has returned to France, there was at least one reason for ignoring the interval. But by the beginning of Act V the Chorus is an established figure of the play, and his absence at this point would have left a puzzling gap in its presentation.

The unusual dependence of *Henry V* upon modes of narrative may be explained by the absence of any serious opposition to the King. As Bolingbroke's lawful heir, Henry V enjoys the double security of moral right and popular approbation; and in this respect is a king unique among Shakespeare's monarchs. Unlike his father, he faces no challenge from mutinous nobles or envious rivals: his title to the crown is undisputed, and his fitness to rule is never questioned. The conspiracy of Grey, Scroop and Cambridge is inspired by French fears of the King, not by any unpopularity with his own subjects, and does not bring him into serious hazard. The plot has no growth: when the audience first hears of the conspiracy it has already been detected, and the King is master of the situation. The general respect felt for him by his subjects is voiced at every level of society; from the Archbishop who acknowledges him as 'full of grace and fair regard' to the swaggering Pistol, who describes the King as 'a bawcock and a heart of gold' and professes a heartfelt love for 'the lovely bully'. This respect is shared by the more judicious of the French king's advisers. The Constable of France knows him to be a fearsome enemy:

> How well supplied with noble counsellors,
> How modest in exception, and withal
> How terrible in constant resolution.
>
> ii. 4. 333–5

The Chorus adds a voice to this general approbation by speaking of Henry as 'the mirror of all Christian kings'; a description adopted in part by the King himself when he assures the French ambassador that he is

> no tyrant, but a Christian king;
> Unto whose grace our passion is as subject
> As is our wretches fetter'd in our prisons.
>
> I. 2. 241–3

This strict restraint of passion means, among other things, that the King is not troubled by the lure of power and ambition which obsessed other Shakespearian monarchs. Within his own kingdom he is secure, and has no other honours to obtain. If he embarks upon a campaign of foreign conquest it is not to gain any personal advantage; and he does not prepare for war with France until the Archbishop has assured him that right and conscience support his claim to the French crown.

His personal blamelessness and political probity have encouraged a belief that in *Henry V* Shakespeare depicted the king of his own ideal. The critical hazards of trying to

separate Shakespeare's private opinions from the varied
body of ideas voiced in his work must be obvious. Shakespeare expresses himself in the imaginative awareness of
the whole play, and not in some attractive feature isolated
by the critic. It may be worth considering whether the
admittedly virtuous character of Henry V could account
for Shakespeare's evident difficulty in bringing his
material to life. Unlike Richard II and Henry IV, the
King is not involved in contradictions of character and
moral identity; and however admirable he may appear by
comparison with them, this integrity of being seems not
to hold the imaginative interest which impels Shakespeare
to create. The most successful of the history-plays owes
much to his imaginative searching into character divided
against itself: a motif which he could not find in the kind
of ideal king which critics have discovered in *Henry V*.
It would appear from this that Shakespeare's conception
of an ideal king—assuming him to have formed such a
conception—and his creative power were at odds; and
that the material of *Henry V* is not fused together because,
without the stimulus of individual conflict, Shakespeare
could not reach the stage of imaginative engagement at
which the poet 'dissolves, diffuses, dissipates, in order to
re-create'. The episodes of *Henry V* in which the play
becomes poetically alive are moments of uncertainty and
doubt in the King, when his virtuousness seems of no
help in solving the moral dilemmas to which he is exposed by kingship.

A more balanced view of the play will find less encouragement to see an ideal king than a figure of folklore
in its central character. Unless the Archbishop is speaking
like a shameless sycophant, his account of the King's
virtues and talents must strain reasonable credulity:

Hear him but reason in divinity,
And, all-admiring, with an inward wish
You would desire the king were made a prelate:
Hear him debate of commonwealth affairs,
You would say it hath been all in all his study:
List his discourse of war, and you shall hear
A fearful battle render'd you in music:
Turn him to any cause of policy,
The Gordian knot of it he will unloose,
Familiar as his garter.

i. i. 38–47

Evidently the audience is to accept this lavish eulogy as a statement of fact, without objecting that in a young man not previously given to study such accomplishments are impossible. But Shakespeare is not asking his audience to suppose that the Hal of Eastcheap has been transformed into this paragon of learning and discretion. In this opening scene of *Henry V* he gives notice that the King is to be clearly dissociated from the Prince of *Henry IV*; not in respect of the riotously misspent youth which the King acknowledges, though with a cryptic suggestion of its usefulness, but in the manner of his transformation to responsible ruler. Instead of maintaining the position he contrives in *Henry IV*, where Hal is made to assume the character of prodigal son for his own undivulged purposes, Shakespeare returns to the traditional account of Hal's unprincipled wildness, and adopts the popular explanation of a completely unpremeditated change of character at the young King's coronation. This silent dropping of an idea devised for the special circumstances of *Henry IV* might be expected, since as a separate play *Henry V* has to contrive its own basis; but in falling back upon folklore Shakespeare rejected a realistic appraisal of Hal's character and motives in favour of a

romantic and familiar one. The fact that this reappraisal
involved a change from a fully organic idea devised by
Shakespeare to a *donnée* of popular belief has its own
significance. The poet is no longer under pressure to
reshape traditional ideas to his own purposes. What we
shall chiefly notice, however, is Shakespeare's abandonment of the realistic position from which the events of
Henry IV are watched and described. If Henry V appears
in the character of an ideal king, this is largely because
Shakespeare is no longer bringing critical discernment to
bear upon the material provided by the chronicles. He
provides a figure of the King in keeping with popular
sentiment and expectation; without comment.

We should not think that Shakespeare could not have
concurred with the popular view of Hal's sudden transformation. Although in *Henry V* Shakespeare adapted
popular tradition to his own purposes by cutting Hal's
character to an entirely new pattern, the resulting figure
of Hal cannot be held to embody his private beliefs
about the behaviour and motives of the historical prince.
The important difference between the two versions of Hal
presented by Shakespeare is that the first of them acts as
representative of a steady critical judgement, seen most
obviously in Hal's quick appreciation of moral truth.
Shakespeare's creative energy is inseparable from the
working of his critical awareness, and what he brings into
being he subjects to a moral scrutiny whose intensity is
proportionate to his creative force. The great diversity and
imaginative range of *Henry IV* demonstrates Shakespeare's
vitality as creator in a play whose characters are exposed to
an unsparing moral examination throughout. To suggest
that Shakespeare might have written a satisfactory play—
whether on Henry V or some other subject—by expressing

popular opinion, ignores the vital aspect of creative activity which consists of questioning the assumptions by which characters attempt to justify themselves. The one episode of *Henry V* which rises clearly above the level of chronicle-history is the scene in which the King examines the moral bases of his authority and realises how uncertain they are.

If *Henry V* cannot claim equality of rank with Shakespeare's previous plays about English history, the poet's evident disinclination to look critically into the King's behaviour and beliefs is chiefly responsible. This does not mean that the King is wilfully or unconsciously mistaken about the moral fitness of his policy, but that Shakespeare makes no attempt to establish through the action what standards of political behaviour the King should adopt. His attitude is settled from the outset, and treated as though it were above criticism; so that even his threat to sack and ravage Harfleur arouses no humanitarian protest within the play. In *Henry IV* Bolingbroke offers an image of royalty which the action proves false by persistently questioning the attitudes he takes up; exposing his fraudulence by ironic parallels with other ambitious rebels, and making implicit the standards of genuine kingship which Bolingbroke cannot reach. The audience is made to see the impostor in a context of authentic standards by which he is condemned, despite his often plausible claims to sovereignty; and is given a critical insight into Bolingbroke's character which he himself does not possess. *Henry V* promotes no critical activity of this kind. Except in the one scene of self-examination, the King does not come under scrutiny. He is uncritically acknowledged and respected by his own people and by the French leaders, and Shakespeare gives him no reason to look into the legality of his title to a throne which should be occupied by Edmund Mortimer. The King has not inherited the talking starling which Hotspur was to have given Bolingbroke. There is in consequence no such working-out of moral standards as Shakespeare contrives through the action of *Henry IV*, and no character to take over Falstaff's satirical function by looking beneath the outward forms of dignity and grandeur. The lack of such critical questioning makes *Henry V* a much less intensely realised play than its predecessor, and a work on which Shakespeare's attention is seldon fully engaged.

The much lower level of critical awareness in *Henry V* is seen in the character of the King himself. In *Henry IV* Hal is the one clear-sighted and undeceived observer in a world of hypocrisy and double-dealing. He does not carry this acute perception with him when he leaves Eastcheap. The treachery of his bosom friend Scroop,

> that didst bear the key of all my counsels,
> That knew'st the very bottom of my soul,
>
> ii. 2. 96f.

takes the King completely by surprise, as though the savage trick he played on Falstaff had come home to roost. Not only is he entirely unprepared for the discovery, but so staggered by the disclosure that he can barely come to terms with his disillusion:

> 'Tis so strange
> That, though the truth of it stands off as gross
> As black and white, my eye will scarcely see it.
>
> ii. 2. 102–4

The Hal of *Henry IV* could not have been so deluded by falsehood: a fact which should make us wonder exactly what kind of profit the King claims to have derived from his irresponsible life about Eastcheap. He has not simply lost his sharp intelligence since becoming king; rather, his lack of perception reflects the lower threshold of awareness that is general in *Henry V*. His previous function as observer, involved in the action yet standing apart from it as moral critic, representing in himself the degraded standards of his father's kingdom yet dissociating himself from Bolingbroke's false authority, enables Shakespeare to represent a complex awareness whose activity is felt throughout *Henry IV*. Hal's sharply discerning judgement would find no place in *Henry V*, which does not challenge the young King with the moral equivocations of Bolingbroke's corrupted world.

Where Bolingbroke attempts to disguise his crimes, his son shows a serious concern to face the moral problems which confront him, in his private life as in his exercise of sovereign power. From the beginning of the play until the victory at Agincourt the King undergoes recurrent crises of belief which threaten to immobilise him if they are not satisfactorily cleared up. The first of these occurs before the King takes the decision to invade France in pursuit of his claim to the French throne. We are perhaps invited to contrast the King's careful and sober enquiry into the moral and legal force of his claim with the contempt for justice displayed by all Shakespeare's earlier aspirants to kingly power. There is opportunity, when the Archbishop speaks of the King's interest in

> his true titles to some certain dukedoms,
> And generally to the crown and seat of France,
> Derived from Edward, his great-grandfather
>
> i. 1. 87–89

to hint at the disregarded issue of the inheritor's title to the English crown stolen by Bolingbroke; but the allusion has no ironic overtones. Instead of raising this issue, Shakespeare allows the King to build upon an unequivocal reference to his 'true titles' by telling the Archbishop to declare 'justly and religiously' whether the Salic law obstructs his claim. At first reading it is difficult to believe that the King's warning against straining and misrepresenting facts—a familiar process in the political machinations of all parties in *Henry IV*—is not another virtuous protestation, meant to recoil upon the speaker; but again Shakespeare's irony is silent. 'God forbid,' the King tells the prelates,

> That you should fashion, wrest, or bow your reading,
> Or nicely charge your understanding soul
> With opening titles miscreate, whose right
> Suits not in native colours with truth.
>
> i. 2. 14–17

The speech turns upon a number of crucial terms—right, truth, conscience, baptism—and upon references to spurious claims which should establish a basis of moral judgement; but in *Henry V* such terms are inert. The King is sincere in wishing to be cleared by religious authority before undertaking war against France, and the Archbishop seems to be offering sincere advice. Because he is acting deliberately, the King is able to reflect dispassionately upon the likely consequences of making war, and to recognise what unforeseen dangers his decision may incur. His warning to the Archbishop admits hazards that are both moral and physical; from neither of which the King can dissociate himself:

> Take heed how you impawn our person,
> How you awake our sleeping sword of war:
> We charge you, in the name of God, take heed.
>
> Ibid., 21–23

It would be wrong to suppose that the King is merely satisfying his conscience over the justice of his claim before declaring war. Whether right is on his side or not, the destructive effects of war between England and France will be so terrible that the responsibility for opening the conflict must daunt any thoughtful ruler. The repeated warning, 'take heed', is not addressed only to the Archbishop: the King must himself be sure that both this advice and his own final decision are not swayed by interests that would condemn his military undertaking from the outset. Two such countries cannot go to war, he tells the Archbishop,

> Without much fall of blood; whose guiltless drops
> Are every one a woe, a sore complaint
> 'Gainst him whose wrongs gives edge unto the swords
> That makes such waste in brief mortality.
>
> Ibid., 25–28

The King is discovering, not for the last time, the loneliness of supreme office, where he must bear the final responsibility for the gravest of decisions. To suggest that he is simply seeking spiritual guidance, and proving his moral superiority over so many earlier Shakespearian kings, is to overlook the nature of the challenge which confronts the King in his attempt to satisfy justice and private conscience: a challenge which his usurping father was not obliged to face. Bolingbroke was driven by a force of personal ambition which made him blind to moral law and contemptuous of its restraints. His son denies himself the impulse of private interest, which provides an immediate spur to action; and feels his way uncertainly towards a judgement formed by weighing legal arguments and material considerations. This respect for moral law and humanity is in itself admirable; but although the outcome of the King's deliberations is never in doubt, we are made to feel an uncertainty and disquiet behind his search for assurance which—in some other dramatic circumstances—might have led to an *impasse*. The undue length of the Archbishop's recital of French history should suggest to any playgoer who remains awake the difficulty of disentangling from such a confusion of facts a plain answer to the King's simple question:

> May I with right and conscience make this claim?
>
> Ibid., 96

Like the Trojan princes in *Troilus and Cressida*, who discover when they try to debate the value of Helen that worth has no fixed standards, the King comes near to finding that right and wrong may be qualities impossible to determine. Shakespeare's plot does not allow his central character to become immobilised by uncertainty of this kind here, though later in the play the King will encounter a greater challenge to the beliefs which impel purposeful action. But this second scene of *Henry V* shows the King in some trouble; not merely obtaining religious approval for the course he intends to follow, but looking for answers to moral problems that are too weighty and complex for any simple solution to be adopted with complete confidence. Rejecting the course of private impulse followed by Bolingbroke does not only mean exchanging crime for legality, as immediately appears, but abandoning the directness of private will for the intricate arguments of moral controversy, from which a clear directive may never emerge.

In the event the King's decision is prompted less by an assured sense of justice than by the eagerness of his advisers to see him in action. The moral justification offered by the Archbishop amounts only to a point of Jewish law quoted from Numbers. On the other side Ely reminds the King persuasively that he is

> in the very May-morn of his youth,
> Ripe for exploits and mighty enterprises.
>
> Ibid., 120f.

Exeter follows this inducement by speaking of the expectation which the King will disappoint if he fails to assert his warlike nature:

> Your brother kings and monarchs of the earth
> Do all expect that you should rouse yourself,
> As did the former lions of your blood.
>
> Ibid., 122–4

For thirty-five lines the King remains silent while the two prelates, Exeter and Westmoreland follow one another in pressing him to decide for war. The passage creates an impression of the King's unwillingness to commit himself to any positive course of action; and another hundred lines pass before he at last yields to persuasion, and announces, 'Now are we well resolved.' His silence and slowness to respond to various forms of emotional pressure can be read as proof of the King's deliberate circumspection; and perhaps this simple interpretation of his behaviour should be accepted. Yet an impression of uncertainty and hesitation remains; to be recalled when later in the play the King's established beliefs undergo a severer and more disabling interrogation.

Whether we are to see some incompletely realised crisis of personal outlook behind the King's questioning of moral right may be open to dispute; but there is no doubt that Scroop's defection, brought to light on the eve of the King's embarkation for France, undermines an area of belief on which much of his private security depends. Beside losing a trusted friend, the King discovers that a central assumption of his outlook is valueless. In this shock of disillusionment he shares the experience of other Shakespearian characters in slightly later plays; of Hamlet and Troilus, who suffer a complete disorientation of private belief when a vital tenet of faith collapses. By discrediting the system of belief which has hitherto guided the King, Scroop's treachery threatens to paralyse his ability to take decisive action. In consequence, it puts the success of the English expedition in hazard. What dumbfounds the King is not the cruelty of his betrayal but the seeming lack of motive in Scroop's treachery. 'He that tempered thee bade thee stand up,' the King tells him,

> Gave thee no instance why thou should'st do treason,
> Unless to dub thee with the name of traitor.
>
> ii. 2. 119f.

Even with the proof in his hands, the King finds it impossible to assimilate the fact of Scroop's broken trust. To accommodate this unthinkable fact his mind must reconstruct its disordered pattern of beliefs upon a new basis; and meanwhile the King is denied the assurance of tried assumptions. 'I will weep for thee,' he tells Scroop;

> For this revolt of thine, methinks, is like
> Another fall of man.
>
> ibid., 141f.

The remark is not simply hyperbolic, but an indication of how profoundly the King's security has been shaken. The full significance of his admission is not seen until it is set beside the Archbishop's reference to the spiritual reflections by which the King 'whipped the offending Adam

out of him' when he succeeded to the throne. The innocence which the King acquired at his accession was both
a freedom from sin and a state of unsuspecting trust, like
that of a newly-made man who had yet to encounter evil.
Scroop has now opened the King's eyes to the existence
of moral corruption in the most unthinkable place and
the most repulsive form. The disclosure strikes at the
roots of the beliefs which have shaped the King's outlook
and character, and so brings his personality under strain.
The demands of the plot do not allow Shakespeare to
develop the situation. At the end of his anguished reproach the King rapidly pulls himself together, commits
the offenders to the course of law, and sets out for France
with a cheerful enthusiasm that belies the shocked
incredulity he has just expressed. The happy assurance of
his belief,

> We doubt not now
> But every rub is smoothed on our way
> Ibid., 187f.

is plainly incompatible with the state of shocked depression which he ascribes to himself less than fifty lines
earlier. So sudden a transformation of outlook is not
accountable in terms of character. It springs from a conflict of interests between the element of historical triumph
that dominates the outward purposes of *Henry V* and the
passages of sombre personal disclosure that give the
King a character at odds with his popular identity. The
sudden change of mood at the end of this scene rules out
the possibility that Shakespeare was trying to combine a
sensitive, introspective mind with the practical, warlike
abilities of a man of action. The two elements do not
combine, but contradict one another. The detection of

Scroop's conspiracy has invited Shakespeare to develop a theme of imaginative interest – soon to be treated at full length in *Hamlet* – to which the positive tone and dramatic intention of *Henry V* give little encouragement. When the demands of the historical plot begin to press upon this imaginative digression, Shakespeare abandons it and returns to his hero's triumphant progress.

Thus, although Shakespeare does not explain how the King rapidly absorbs the double shock of Scroop's treachery and a disillusioning of private belief, he lets it appear that the King's resolution has been severely challenged, and that he has fought off a well-timed and potentially demoralising attack upon his royal purposes. In France he is to meet further challenges; not in the simple form of physical or tactical hazards which he has ample courage to resist, but in more insidious threats to his moral assurance. The first of these is presented by the French herald, who issues his challenge when the King knows himself to be heavily outnumbered, and his small army weakened by sickness. This military disadvantage is serious enough to give the King some anxiety, and Mountjoy's speech attempts to exploit this natural sense of misgiving by suggesting that rash leadership and insulting arrogance are about to be fittingly punished in the repulse of an ill-considered military adventure. 'England shall repent his folly, see his weakness, and admire our sufferance,' Mountjoy promises impressively;

> Bid him therefore consider of his ransom, which must proportion the losses we have borne, the subjects we have lost, the disgrace we have digested: which in weight to re-answer, his pettiness would bow under.

iii. 6. 131–5

The verbal assault on the King's morale is most damaging

in its final comment: 'Tell him, for conclusion, he hath betrayed his followers.' The implication that he has behaved like Scroop might itself unsettle the King; and the knowledge that a sick and enfeebled army has been brought into peril through his decisions could check his confidence with the disheartening suggestion that his invasion of France was a foolhardy mistake. In the depressing circumstances of Mountjoy's challenge, the sober warning that the French are about to take full revenge for the hurts done to them must have an ominous ring of likelihood. The King's compliment to Mountjoy, 'Thou dost thine office fairly,' admits that the threat has been given teeth. But the form of the King's answer, which begins as though unconcernedly by asking the herald his name, proves him unshaken:

> If we may pass, we will; if we be hinder'd,
> We shall your tawny ground with your red blood
> Discolour.
>
> Ibid., 166–8

This calmly defiant statement of purpose disposes of Mountjoy's challenge to the King's belief in his cause; but as night falls upon his uneasy army a different form of threat begins to take shape. Its nature is suggested in the fourth speech of the Chorus, whose first thirty lines constitute an outstanding piece of mood-writing, evoking through physical description a sense of the sluggishness and heavy foreboding that take hold of exhausted men in the night-watch before battle. Their reluctance to face the morning is felt in the disquieting sounds that accompany the dragging passage of time:

> The country cocks do crow, the clocks do toll,
> And the third hour of drowsy morning name.
>
> IV. 15–16

The men who undergo this exposure to fear themselves
become part of the nightmarish scene which daunts the
army's spirit; seeming insubstantial and ghastly in the
moonlight as

> their gesture sad
> Investing lank-lean cheeks and war-worn coats
> Presenteth them unto the gazing moon
> So many horrid ghosts.
>
> IV. 25–28

The appearance of this emaciated, almost spectral army
suggests an already defeated force haunting the site of a
military disaster. This opening section of the speech
makes it difficult to believe that the King will be able to
invigorate his depressed and sickly army, even to the
point where they might offer resistance to the French. It
also suggests that the sense of superstitious misgiving
and dread to which the speech appeals will be awakened
in the King, taking advantage of the night to magnify
the anxiety which he must feel, and to undermine his
resolution with the chill of fear. But in fact when the King
is mentioned at line 29 the tone of the speech at once
changes, gathering energy and confidence as though
breaking away from spiritual oppression. As he passes
through his army the King radiates cheerfulness, thawing
the frozen courage of his men:

> That every wretch, pining and pale before,
> Beholding him, plucks comfort from his looks.
> A largess universal like the sun
> His liberal eye doth give to every one.
>
> IV. 41–44

With this final effect of sunrise, the whole Chorus completes an imaginative movement from the forebodings of
an uneasy dream, in which the sleeper is attacked by

instinctive fears held back by the waking mind, to the renewal of confidence that is symbolised rather than encouraged by the return of daylight. The deeper implications of the speech are that the King has himself been made to feel the hopelessness which drains strength and will to fight from his army; and that he has fought off the instinctive fears which take hold of tired men during the uncertainty of darkness.

A more disturbing challenge now confronts him. As he samples the morale of his army through his conversation with Bates and Williams, the King discovers that his men regard him as one of themselves in wishing to save his neck whatever happens. 'He may show what outward courage he will,' Bates remarks simply,

> but I believe, as cold a night as 'tis, he could wish himself in Thames up to the neck . . . so we were quit here.
>
> iv. 1. 115–18

His remark implies a total rejection of the noble standards which direct the King's behaviour; in particular his conduct as a soldier. Bates, in his forthright valuation of life, feels no respect for noble reputation: he will fight lustily for the King, but with the entirely realistic intention of keeping a whole skin; and without supposing that love of honour runs very deep. If the King enjoys his present danger, Bates continues, 'then I would he were here alone'; he would then be ransomed, and 'a many poor men's lives' would be spared. Hitherto, in his pursuit of military honour, the King has ignored the fate of the ordinary fighting-man whose uncomplaining service buttresses great reputations and famous victories. He is now being made to acknowledge how much such achievements depend upon the loyalty and personal

sacrifice of men too poor and unimportant to merit
ransoming; and who, unlike their leaders, cannot expect
a painless outcome to defeat. Pushed home, this recognition must call into question assumptions that are fundamental to the King's active direction of an invading army;
but the interrogation of his beliefs does not stop here.
When the King answers Bates by asserting that he would
be content to die in his sovereign's company, 'his cause
being just and his quarrel honourable', Williams cuts in
with an unanswerable comment,

> That's more than we know.
> Ibid., 130

The sense of the remark may be simply that issues of
this kind are above the head of the common man; but the
King can hardly avoid the suggestion that the problem of
his moral right to invade France is being raised again, in
the form of a direct challenge. Bates has no wish to hear
the matter discussed: it is enough for him to know that
they are the King's subjects, bound to obedience whether
or not his cause is just, and so not implicated in the guilt
of wrongful proceeding:

> If his cause be wrong, our obedience to the king wipes the
> crime of it out of us.
>
> Ibid., 133f.

Williams takes up this point and develops it with some
energy; arguing that unless the King has right on his
side he will have a heavy reckoning to make at Judgement Day, when all the bodies dismembered in battle will
join together to witness against him, crying, 'We died at
such a place.' To refute this argument might not be easy;
but as Williams continues he shifts attention from the
King's guilty responsibility for the deaths of his subjects,

and speaks about the weight of private sin in soldiers who die unshriven. This change of subject allows the King to ignore the question of his general responsibility in a doubtful cause, and to answer only the suggestion that he is to blame when his soldiers die in battle with misdeeds on their consciences. This is a comparatively easy matter. 'If they die unprovided,' he tells Williams at the end of an extended reply,

> no more is the king guilty of their damnation than he was before guilty of those impieties for the which they are now visited. Every subject's duty is the king's; but every subject's soul is his own.
>
> Ibid., 180–4

The King has evaded the major issue; but the unanswered problem of his right to commit men to battle where justice cannot be determined continues to challenge his immediate purposes. The question drops out of sight, yet the discordant note introduced by Williams's comment, 'That's more than we know', has not been silenced. The implications of his remark reach beyond the limits of this scene. Other Shakespearean kings are disturbed by their inability to assume the whole identity of sovereign, either through personal shortcomings or by reason of illegality. No such bar stands between Henry V and the crown; instead, he is assailed by moral doubts over the nature and force of royal authority which none of his predecessors have shared. Where Richard II and Bolingbroke struggle to possess the royal identity which neither adequately fills, Henry V is allowed to capture this elusive reality; only to discover that its premises of spiritual authority are suspect. The King is prepared to go some way towards admitting that his human condition is like that of any other man; though in the circumstances

191

of his disguise the statement, 'I think the king is but a man, as I am', may be equivocal: the speaker is the King, and Bates is not such a man as he is. Taken at its face value, the remark shows a modest self-awareness that safeguards the King against any false estimate of his royal nature:

> all his senses have but human conditions: his ceremonies laid by, in his nakedness he appears but a man.
>
> Ibid., 104–6

Again there may be some equivocation: the King appears but a man, though in fact much more. Yet if we assume that the King is speaking plainly and sincerely, refusing to claim any special virtue or implanted power for himself, there must remain some quiet assumption of invested authority and right which are his title to govern and command. In the discussion with Bates and Williams this assumption comes under severe pressure. Beside learning how cynically the common soldier regards the practice of ransoming noble prisoners, the King discovers that his men believe him to be human in a more depreciatory sense than he had intended. Williams admits that the King has declared his refusal to be ransomed, but scorns to take the announcement seriously:

> Ay, he said so, to make us fight cheerfully; but when our throats are cut, he may be ransomed, and we ne'er the wiser.
>
> Ibid., 199–201

When the King tries to make an objection defending his own good faith, he touches off an outburst of contempt and indignation from Williams, who has evidently brooded over the inequitable difference between the noble and the plebeian terms of service. 'You pay him then!' he advises the King derisively;

THE TRUE INHERITOR

That's a perilous shot out of an elder-gun, that a poor and a
private displeasure can do against a monarch. You may as well
go about to turn the sun to ice with fanning in his face with
a peacock's feather.

Ibid., 203

In this tense situation the common touch acquired by
Hal about Eastcheap seems to desert him; and in another
moment the King has the promise of a fight on his hands.
By making a personal issue out of this frank appreciation
of his character and motives, the King is being less than
fair to Williams, who has thrown some startling light
upon the outlook of the common soldier. But the King is
understandably shocked by the disclosure of this cynical
contempt for the standards of honourable behaviour, and
he reacts impulsively against an attempt to ridicule and
discredit a vital part of his personal faith. Eastcheap seems
not to have taught him that the common man sees war
without the context of heroic ideals that uplifts the King.
To realise on the eve of a decisive battle, where without
courage and dedication he must expect his army to be overwhelmed, that common judgement sees him striking a
noble posture only to impress his soldiers, is another disillusioning experience which threatens to weaken the
King's resolution. In an earlier scene Gower shows that he
has learned to live with the fact that the world is easily
deluded by the swaggering boastfulness of a Pistol. He
tells Fluellen:

what a beard of the general's cut and a horrid suit of the camp
will do among foaming bottles and ale-washed wits, is
wonderful to be thought on. But you must learn to know
such slanders of the age, or else you may be marvellously
mistook.

iii. 6. 78–83

The impulse behind this realistic appreciation is not readily associated with the towering hyperbole of the Chorus's references to war, which invite the audience to adopt much the same uncritical attitude towards soldiering as Gower warns Fluellen against. A good part of the dissatisfaction which *Henry V* arouses derives from its failure to take up a consistent position in respects of this kind. If the audience follows the promptings of the Chorus, who seems to speak directly on the poet's behalf, it will not be prepared to question the rapturous approval expressed in his second speech, where 'silken dalliance in the wardrobe lies',

> and honour's thought
> Reigns solely in the breast of every man.
> II. 3f.

Pistol's cowardly braggartism, Gower's warning against those who bring shame on their times, and William's angry scorn for the pretentiousness of 'honour's thought', proves that a satirical impulse is also at work upon the matter of the play, and perhaps upon Shakespeare. The open dispute with Williams leaves the King badly shaken; and in the soliloquy which follows he shows himself for the first time doubtful of his royal authority and of the dignity which it confers upon him. The speech touches on a theme found elsewhere in Shakespeare, of the simple pleasures denied to kings yet granted to the poorest subject; but here the familiar commentary is sharpened by an angry anatomising of the privileged treatment which sets the king apart from the common body of men:

> And what art thou, thou idol ceremony?
> What kind of god art thou, that suffer'st more

Of mortal griefs than do thy worshippers?
What are thy rents? what are thy comings-in?
O ceremony, show me but thy worth!
What is thy soul of adoration?
Art thou aught else but place, degree, and form,
Creating awe and fear in other men?

iv. 1. 246–53

This sceptical bitterness is a mood not previously heard from the King; but he has only now recognised that his unique status rests upon this seemingly illusory basis. 'By this admission Shakespeare reintroduces a theme central to *Richard II* and *Henry IV*, though represented only intermittently in *Henry V*. The two earlier kings pursued an idea of royal greatness which neither succeeded in realising. Bolingbroke's son has no need to strain after the identity counterfeited by his father, for he is king by right both of due inheritance and of natural authority; but in his soliloquy before Agincourt he is made to discover the insubstantiality of the office which Bolingbroke destroyed himself to possess.

Like the disillusioning disclosure of Scroop's motiveless treachery, the King's recognition that only the trivial process of ceremony distinguishes him from other men does not fit naturally into the play outlined and presented by the Chorus. It seems worth remarking that the passages of *Henry V* which reveal the King's private feelings, and which were not drawn from Shakespeare's source-material, convey an impression of scepticism and disquiet strongly alien to the generally optimistic spirit of the play. These conflicting purposes are made to serve a single dramatic end when the King is first impeded by doubts and later released from his hesitation, triumphing over an opposing army and his own uncertainties in the

195

same affirmation of self-confidence; yet the sense of disparity remains between the plain terms of patriotic chronicle-play and the occasional passages of satirical inquiry in which Shakespeare's imaginative commitment is more positively felt. Possibly we should regard *Henry V* essentially as a chronicle-play to which Shakespeare has given high rhetorical colour through the speeches of the Chorus, and the less usual interest of dramatic insight into the hero's private experience. But it seems a misreading of Shakespeare's intentions to suppose that the King's argument with Bates and Williams, and the destructive analysis of ceremony that follows, were meant to supplement the source-material of the chronicles. This scene appears to have forced itself upon the play, insisting upon a hearing without respect to the spirit and purpose of its dramatic context. If Shakespeare's audience was prepared to accept a new play along the general lines of *The Famous Victories*, his imagination was evidently unwilling to adapt itself to this limited project. Where Shakespeare becomes imaginatively engaged in the situations of *Henry V*, the ideas which he develops are irreconcilable with the sense of lofty exaltation and splendid achievement which the Chorus asks the audience to expect of the play.

This imaginative engagement is strongly felt in the images of fixity and inaction which recur throughout *Henry V*. In a play concerned with campaigns and battles the predominant mood might be one of energetic movement; and a persistent interest in stagnation and inertia could indicate that the physical events of the play did not contain the centre of imaginative attention. This seems the case here. Suggestions of an immobilised will, hard to set in motion, are present from the opening scenes.

Although the King's refusal to be hurried into a declaration of war does credit to his moral circumspection, some of the terms he uses carry implications of a reluctance to move at all. His warning to the Archbishop,

> Take heed . . .
> How you awake our sleeping sword of war;
> > i. 2. 21f.

seems to admit a personal drowsiness which his counsellors urge to shake off: 'Awake remembrance . . . rouse yourself.' The Archbishop's promptings include a curious reference to the English victory at Cressy won by half an army, while the rest of the King's forces looked on unused,

> All out of work, and cold for action.
> > i. 2. 114

The speaker's immediate intention is to suggest the laughable ease of this victory over the French; but the image of inactivity suggests a force which has only partly stirred itself out of lassitude. The idea of awakened vigour struggling to free itself of a clogging inertia is expressed later by the King, in remarking to Erpingham that when 'the mind is quickened',

> The organs, though defunct and dead before,
> Break up their drowsy grave, and newly move
> With casted slough and fresh legerity.
> > iv. 1. 21–23

The remark follows a scene in the French camp which epitomises the languor and boredom of enforced idleness. The trivial bickering of the French lords, their wit as jaded as their yawning assurance of easy victory, is interrupted again and again by weary complaints about the sluggish passing of time— 'Will it never be morning?' 'What a long night is this!'—which involve the audience in the same stagnation of spirit. Unlike the English, the French lords have no respect for their leader, and no expectation that his boastful promises will be translated into action. 'Doing is activity, and he will still be doing,' the Constable comments of the Dauphin; to which Orleans replies damningly,

> He never did harm, that I heard of.
>
> iii. 7. 101

'Nor will do none tomorrow,' the Constable forecasts; but on the morning of the battle he himself assures the French lords that they need barely exert themselves to overwhelm so petty a foe:

> There is not work enough for all our hands.
>
> iv. 2. 19

The theme of inertia and futile activity continues to occupy Shakespeare's imagination as the Constable speaks of the throngs of servants and country people who swarm about the French army 'in unnecessary action', and suggests that these unwarlike followers could rout the English without help,

> Though we upon this mountain's basis by
> Took stand for idle speculation.
>
> Ibid., 30f.

This notion of idle bystanders recalls the Archbishop's description of the force withheld from action at Cressy. Here the French army is to see action, but in an engagement too brief to warm them thoroughly. 'What's to say?' the Constable asks, feeling that the occasion does not rate any rousing exhortation;

> A very little little let us do,
> And all is done.
>
> Ibid., 33f.

The whole tendency of his address is to suggest a task so undemanding that the French need hardly trouble to brace themselves for battle: merely to make an appearance in the field will assure victory. Encouraged to be indolent and lazily casual, they deserve Grandpré's rebuke, 'Why do you stay so long?' though the description of the English which he brings must give them more cause to remain relaxed. His account of men and beasts in a state of dispirited lethargy and exhaustion has a poetic power which indicates an unusual degree of imaginative commitment on Shakespeare's part:

> The horsemen sit like fixed candlesticks,
> With torch-staves in their hand; and their poor jades
> Lob down their heads, dropping the hides and hips,
> The gum down-roping from their pale-dead eyes,
> And in their pale dull mouths the gimmal'd bit
> Lies foul with chaw'd grass, still and motionless.
>
> Ibid., 45–50

Grandpré's report does not tally with the audience's view of the English army, which, however depleted, is in good heart and ready for battle; but his speech should not be read as an attempt to boost French morale. Whatever function it serves in respect of the plot of *Henry V*, within the poetic design of the play this extended metaphor of unresponsive apathy has an importance not determined by its part in the dramatic story. Because the French discover that Grandpré was badly mistaken, his picture of an army sunk in torpor does not cease to be imaginatively effective: it continues to exert the pressure of a fully realised concept upon the structure of ideas which Shakespeare builds up. While the plot moves towards its climax in military action, the overthrow of a great army by a weak and outnumbered force, the imaginative attention of *Henry V* pursues its own dissociated course by suggesting enervation and idleness on both sides. Westmoreland's wish to be reinforced by

> But one ten thousand of those men in England
> That do no work today!
>
> iv. 3. 17f.

is taken from Holinshed but placed appositely in the context of Shakespeare's unheroic battle-scenes, which give more prominence to Pistol's service as 'brave, vaillant, et trés distingué seigneur' than to the King's active personal contribution to the victory. It is curious that of all Shakespeare's stage battles, the most glorious for English audiences should be represented by the efforts of an illiterate braggart to extort ransom from a spineless coward; and a curious contradiction of the impulse that makes the Chorus speak with awed respect of

> the very casques
> That did affright the air at Agincourt.
>
> I. 13f.

The apologies offered by the Chorus for the play's unworthy and inadequate attempts to bring Agincourt before the audience are not out of place; though what might need pardoning is the choice of ignoble and contemptible figures to represent the contending forces, and not a failure to give these scenes the heroic magnitude they deserve. The plea made in the first Chorus,

> Think, when we talk of horses, that you see them
> Printing their proud hoofs i' the receiving earth;
>
> I. 26f.

is immediately effective; but the suggestions of noble endeavour in the speeches of the Chorus are only faintly borne out in the action. This splendid image of horses, and the associations of nobility which it evokes, have no place in the Agincourt scenes. The exhausted mounts described by Grandpré, broken-spirited and ill-conditioned, are more fairly representative of the terms of debased grandeur in which we are obliged to see much of the battle.

A tendency to depreciate the importance of Agincourt is felt again in a suggestion that one of the armies at least is barely substantial; a paper force which a puff of wind will disperse. The Constable sees the English as a poor, starved band whose feeble appetite for battle will be crushed by the mere appearance of the French host,

> Leaving them but the shales and husks of men.
>
> iv. 2. 18

'Let us but blow on them,' he proposes to the French lords,

> The vapour of our valour will o'erturn them.
>
> Ibid., 24

The suggestion proves ironic, and French valour as vaporous as the Constable inadvertently admits; but his image retains a poetic force which the irony does not neutralise. The outcome of battle seems to confirm that a paper army is in the field, and that although misapplied to the English these scornful terms are dramatically relevant. But it is not easy to transfer the sense of such forceful images to the French. When Grandpré describes the dwindled and impoverished state of the English army,

> Big Mars seems bankrupt in their beggar'd host,
> And faintly through a rusty beaver peeps;
>
> Ibid., 43f.

embodying in 'peeps' the frightened reluctance of the English troops to face a hopeless situation, he stamps a clear impression of shaken morale which cannot be erased by making allowance for prejudice. 'Description cannot suit itself in words,' he concludes, doing Shakespeare less than justice,

> To demonstrate the life of such a battle
> In life so lifeless as it shows itself.
>
> Ibid., 54f.

Grandpré might be making a satirical parody of the apologies offered by the Chorus for the dramatic inadequacies of the play. His speech certainly makes it difficult for an audience to retain a respectful image of the army through which the King must prove his great-hearted courage and resolute will. The French view of his forces as a thoroughly demoralised army, whose soldiers are empty effigies of men waiting to be bowled over, is not simply accountable as an over-confident error. On the English side the common soldiers are not alone in feeling the outcome of battle already decided by the great numerical superiority of the French. Exeter's comment,

> There's five to one; besides, they are all fresh
>
> iv. 3. 4

is a muted admission of fear confirmed by Salisbury: ''Tis a fearful odds.' In the temporary absence of the King, confidence does not hold up against the intimidating threats of 'most assured overthrow' which Mountjoy repeats once more before the battle. The King himself must be source and mainstay of his army's courage, fighting back the sense of inferiority expressed in Westmoreland's wish for reinforcements, and compelling them to believe in a victory which will make St Crispin's Day famous in the annals of war. The great challenge which confronts him is not so much the prospect of defeat as the task of transforming a small army, wearied and dispirited to the point of collapse, into a vigorous and self-assured fighting force capable of destroying an enemy several times larger than itself. This transformation must begin within the King. His natural buoyancy has been checked by Williams's contempt for the code of honourable behaviour which must sustain the King, and by his own realisation of the worthlessness of ceremony. His prayer, 'Not today,' admits a deeper sense of unease originating in his father's crime, which might now be avenged in the ruin and humiliation of Bolingbroke's heir. That the King's physical courage is equal to the hazards of his exposed military position is not enough to secure him: his resolution is under attack from more insidious and demoralising forms of uncertainty. Unless he can overcome these misgivings within himself and reanimate his men, the army will remain sunk in the exhausted apathy which Grandpré describes, to be swept away with no more effort than the Constable calls for.

Thus it would be wrong to regard Grandpré as a prejudiced or wilfully optimistic observer; though his picture of an abject and inert English force cannot be accepted quite literally. We are not to suppose that the army looks as spiritless as Grandpré suggests, but to see his images of lifeless apathy representing a state of moral defeat in which fear takes body and mind captive. To this extent his speech is not 'true'; but its imaginative associations illuminate a level of meaning below the plane of dramatic events, where physical happenings acquire the significance of metaphor. The demoralised army which is made to exist imaginatively in Grandpré's speech has such a significance, chiefly for the King who should command its now immobilised power. It indicates the particular danger of the situation which confronts him, and the particular urgency of the need to release his forces from the sickly, trance-like paralysis of spirit which transfixes them. The King answers this crucial challenge in his address to the army, heartening his men by making their small numbers a point of noble credit, and then leading them to inflict a disastrous defeat upon a mangled and bewildered French host.

With Agincourt the play reaches its dramatic climax, and the King undergoes the last and severest of the personal crises which test his abilities as sovereign. He has now fought free of the impeding doubts that repeatedly threaten to clog and hamper vigorous action; and after his culminating triumph over irresolution and inertia we might expect this running theme of *Henry V* to drop out of sight. But if the King has done with the subject, the play has not. In Act V the theme is re-introduced by Burgundy, in one of the long set speeches that characterise the play, supplying background comment rather than developing the action. Burgundy's topic, the wild and neglected state of France brought about by war, invites him to describe the desolation of a countryside left to grow unrestrained and unkempt. Among several curious features of this long and impressive speech is the sense of concern for France, which the audience is induced to share with Burgundy. Hitherto the play has treated the French with a good deal of contempt, openly suggesting that the devastation of their country is a well-deserved punishment for which the audience should feel no pity. By intervening between the combatants, Burgundy now reintroduces the impulse of compassionate feeling exiled by war, and turns attention to the productive labour of cultivation—human as well as agricultural—which warfare has interrupted for so long. Yet although his purpose is entirely constructive—both a knitting-together of his shattered country, and a peaceful alliance of the warring kingdoms—his speech limits attention to the widespread neglect of the French countryside, whose untended fields either waste themselves in unharvested crops or run wild, reverting to uncultivated nature. Part of Burgundy's appeal is directed against this purposeless wasting of creative energy; a protest which, in a long view of the dramatic series about to be concluded, may be read as a moral indictment of the causes which have led to such unproductive spending of human potential. But in his picture of unpopulated farms, where the plough rusts and the scythe lies unused, Burgundy evokes a melancholy impression of a deserted countryside where nothing moves, and weeds smother an abandoned cultivation:

> All her husbandry doth lie on heaps,
> Corrupting in its own fertility.
> Her vine, the merry cheerer of the heart,
> Unpruned dies; her hedges even-pleach'd,
> Like prisoners wildly overgrown with hair,
> Put forth disorder'd twigs; her fallow leas
> The darnel, hemlock and rank fumitory
> Doth root upon, while that the coulter rusts
> That should deracinate such savagery;
> The even mead, that erst brought sweetly forth
> The freckled cowslip, burnet, and green clover,
> Wanting the scythe, all uncorrected, rank,
> Conceives by idleness, and nothing teems
> But hateful docks, rough thistles, kecksies, burrs.
>
> v. 2. 39–52

This deeply felt appeal has rightly attracted a good deal of critical comment. Its greatest interest lies perhaps in its

humanitarian plea for the useful and creative impulses
that are frustrated by war. Burgundy is not concerned
only for the plight of French agriculture, whose natural
riches are running to waste, but for the children who are
left to grow up in the same wildness, without education
or kindly training. They do not learn, he observes,

> The sciences that should become our country,
> But grow like savages, as soldiers will
> That nothing do but meditate on blood.
> Ibid., 58–60

This reference to soldiers suggests the larger scope of
Burgundy's purpose. France is not alone in feeling the
harmful consequences of prolonged war. The speech
should make both sides aware of the wasteful and un-
natural courses into which man's energies are diverted
when he devotes himself to carnage and destruction, and
neglects the vital task of cultivating himself. The picture
of a countryside reverting to wildness, where the imple-
ments that should 'deracinate . . . savagery' lie untouched,
provides a metaphor of the condition which supervenes
when the ferocious impulses of man's natural being
take charge. War has given full licence to instincts which
humanity should discipline and restrain; and Burgundy
warns both combatants of a general danger to the civilised
life of both countries if they continue to develop man's
natural violence at the expense of his creative potentiality.
The 'hateful docks, rough thistles, kecksies, burrs'
which have displaced the pleasant and useful cultivated
growth of the meadows characterise the harsh, unproductive savagery which is ready to usurp the proper place of
the kindliness by which man is nourished.

The mixture of entreaty and warning in Burgundy's

speech has no parallel in Shakespeare's earlier history-plays. For the first time a strong moral rebuke is being uttered against war, for its encouragement of man's natural inclination towards brutishness, and for its destruction of the ordered life which he arduously brings about by civilising and cultivating the natural wildness of himself and his setting. It has some significance that such a speech should occur in the last play of a long series. In a chronological view of English history, the long upheaval of civil war under Henry VI and Richard III remains to be undergone; and if Burgundy's plea is effective in securing peace at this juncture, it has no lasting effect upon those who govern. It may be necessary to insist again that Shakespeare's purposes are best understood from the chronological order of his plays, and not from the historical sequence of the kings whom they depict. To recognise this is to appreciate the significance of Burgundy's appeal against the savagery of war in the last act of Shakespeare's final history-play. A genre which has served his imaginative need for nearly a decade is about to be discarded; and the long series to conclude with the achievement of settled peace between old enemies. The final speech of the Chorus admits the turbid aftermath of Henry V's conquest, 'which oft our stage hath shown'; but the contract of marriage between Henry and Katherine in the closing episode of the play represents a union of warring opposites whose imaginative purpose must be clear.

The positive outcome of *Henry V* has some general significance as the imaginative solution of interests which have occupied Shakespeare's attention since *Henry VI*. It has also a local importance associated with Burgundy's speech. Like Grandpré's description of the English army, the picture of a neglected French countryside evokes a pervasive sense of inactivity and hopeless abandonment. The vines are unpruned, the hedges untrimmed, and swarming weeds defy the scythe; the coulter rusts, and the fertile soil 'conceives by idleness': giving growth to seeds scattered by the wind. The running theme of inertia pursued throughout the play finds this further expression in a scene parallel to the description of an army immobilised by apathy. Again nothing is being done: the wasted luxuriance of crops, and the wild growth of plants enriched by their own decaying fruit cry out for cultivation and tending; but nothing seems likely to overcome the inertia of neglect. It is to this purpose that Burgundy speaks, asking

> What rub or what impediment there is,
>
> Ibid., 33

why peace should not be restored to a country so cruelly ravaged by war? He appears to stand in the same relationship to the neglected kingdom which he describes as the King to his paralysed army; assuming responsibility for its survival, and undertaking the task of breaking the spell which locks up its energies. Although Burgundy's speech can be allowed very little dramatic importance, it has an imaginative function similar to that of Grandpré's report, which it resembles in literary character. Alternation between fixity and vigorous movement, or between immobilised uncertainty and decisive action, is a marked element of the poetic design of *Henry V*. At several points of the play the King's progress is checked by doubts which render him incapable of carrying out his purposes. At each point he manages to shake off this moral paralysis and to assert himself positively. These points form the dramatic cruces of *Henry V*, a play more closely concerned with the inner experience of its central character than any other of the Histories. In the last of these crises the King's transformation of a thoroughly demoralised army into a confident fighting-force leads to the dramatic climax of the play: a final rejection of uncertainty, and a release of pent-up forces which sweep away the great threat which had daunted them.

The more immediate interest of Burgundy's speech is that, under cover of an appeal for France, it brings back the recurrent ideas of apathy and idleness. We expect this challenge to be met, as before, by a thrust of vigorous activity which breaks through the clogging depression and sets impeded life in motion again. So far as the dramatic circumstances allow this impulse of reinvigorating purpose to be represented, it is suggested in the King's wooing of Katherine and the political settlement which concludes the play. The wooing shows the King for the first time in a light-hearted, even frivolous mood; and the sombre emotional colour of Burgundy's speech is relieved by the playfulness of what follows. It would be absurd to argue that a scene as shallow and perfunctory in its dialogue could carry any imaginative conviction; but Shakespeare's intention of giving the last of the Histories the form of a happy ending makes itself apparent. Peace, political harmony and marriage are together to set a term to the waste and upheaval of war, and to allow the neglected arts of civilisation to be practised again. On this note the play and the historical series close.

But such an ending cannot resolve the interests which *Henry V* voices most strongly. It may justify the spirit of elation and confidence injected into the play by the Chorus; but those speeches are not compounded of rapturous exclamation alone. They admit as though for the author a sense of inadequacy and flagging invention which requires the audience to share the work of bringing heroic figures and momentous occasions to life. If these repeated appeals to the audience to work their thoughts are intended seriously, they are not prompted by the physical limitations of Shakespeare's playhouse, but by the evident unwillingness of his imagination to give full reality to the resplendent figures which the Chorus describes. The action of the play gives being to less noble characters: to a king whose royal dignity is compromised by the treachery of a trusted friend and by doubts of his own authority; to common soldiers who fight without belief in the justice of the King's cause, and to cowardly braggarts who bring disgrace on their times. Against the unsettled creative impulse that produces figures of this unexalted kind, the lyrical excitement of the Chorus cannot assert itself to much purpose. His speeches, which express rather a wish than a promise to realise heroic conceptions in dramatic form, provide a generally misleading idea of the play to which he acts as presenter.

Because the play lacks the consistent driving energy that is vital to drama, we may suppose that the apology in the first Chorus for 'the flat unraised spirits' which have produced *Henry V* is something more than a modest formality. If Shakespeare had written a play below his usual standards, we should not expect him to be unaware of its shortcomings. An impression that *Henry V* is a laboured work is confirmed by every appeal to the audience to make good its deficiencies by an imaginative effort of their own. It could seem not merely that Shakespeare recognised how much he had left undone, but that he acknowledged how laborious his task had been by suggesting, through the Chorus, the kind of intense mental concentration required of his audience. It then becomes a matter of critical interest that the central character of *Henry V* is himself repeatedly obstructed by difficulties which he cannot overcome without a determined act of will. These checks to the King's purpose seem to reflect the course of a struggle on Shakespeare's part to write a play whose mood and character were at odds with his growing inclination to question the humanist assumptions which a vital part of himself accepts, as does the King. At this level of interpretation the play is seen acting out a conflict between the King's belief in the essential nobility of man—raised to its highest power in his own majesty—and a realistic acknowledgement of man's ignoble behaviour, which the King must learn to face or 'be marvellously mistook'. Gower can be familiar with the slanders of the age without putting his constancy in hazard; but Shakespeare's central character is a man not previously exposed to the disillusioning fact of human corruption, and his discoveries throw a severe strain upon his private faith. Scroop's betrayal of trust shocks him profoundly; but he is more damagingly shaken by learning that although the common soldiers are ready to fight for him, they do not concern themselves with his cause and are openly contemptuous of the honourable standards which he professes. At this point of the play, where the King yields to scepticism in a scornful analysis of his majesty, he seems about to adopt a position that would deny all dignity to man and to acknowledge himself leader of a raiding-party disguised as a quest for honour and justice. The force of the sceptical argument which confronts him is great enough to immobilise the King. At this crucial point of *Henry V*, where the sense of imaginative commitment is strongest, Shakespeare himself seems to be involved in the King's struggle to assert the positive belief that Williams's scornfully realistic judgement is trying to discredit; and to share the troubled uncertainty which he projects upon his central character.

A play whose poetic integrity is so doubtful resists the kind of interpretative criticism that can be usefully applied to a work which has consistent imaginative purpose. For this reason *Henry V* must remain a frustrating play. It declares contradictory interests, and does not maintain any single well-marked line of development. The popular opinion that it should be read as a splendid patriotic chronicle finds support in the Chorus's speeches and the King's address before Agincourt, but ignores the pointed evidence of an opposite impulse which calls heroic values into question. To argue that this sceptical purpose supplies the main energy of *Henry V* invites the same kind of objection; that much of the writing is fired by an enthusiastic acceptance of the values which elsewhere Shakespeare seems inclined to repudiate. Since the Chorus stands outside the play proper, we might perhaps discount the exalted feeling which his speeches inject into the work; seeing his function as an attempt to offset the satirical impulse which threatens heroic achievement in the play. In a critical summing-up of *Henry V* we may be finally influenced by the fact that while its heroic values form the subject of high rhetorical commentary, its doubts and scepticism are enacted in the few scenes that have the intensity of imaginative engagement.

In its treatment of the identity of king, which is a major theme of these plays, *Henry V* reveals a considerable shift from the outlook of *Richard II*. Richard's failure to assume more than the majestic appearance of kingship does not discredit the reality of the role he wishes to

play: his own weaknesses as a man, and not some insubstantiality in the conception of kingly majesty and
power, brings about the collapse of his unconscious
imposture. In *Henry V* Shakespeare suggests an almost
opposite state of affairs. The King possesses all the
qualities of sovereignty, both natural and acquired; his
legitimacy is not in doubt, he has an exemplary respect for
justice, and is well-loved by his subjects. The player is
ready; but the identity of king threatens to fall to pieces
as he assumes it. His role must take its basis upon the
innate dignity and nobility of man, raised in the king
to godlike splendour as he personifies man's implanted
sovereignty in its most explicit form. For Henry V,
trained and conditioned by humanist doctrines, this basis
begins to crumble with the disclosure of unmotivated
evil in Scroop, whose treachery affects the King like
'another fall of man'. His comment is imaginatively
just; and this discovery that individual man is not a
creature of nobly generous impulses throws into doubt
the conceptions of kingly majesty and splendour raised
upon this mistaken assumption. The King does not need
the accusation relayed by Mountjoy at their first encounter,

Tell him, for conclusion, he hath betrayed his followers
iii. 6. 140f.

to appreciate how dangerously his beliefs may have
misled him. His own experience, sharpened by Williams's
insistence that the King will look to his personal safety
like any other man, suggest how trustfully he has judged
the nature which he shares with his men-at-arms. In his
soliloquy he rejects in disgust the external forms of
sovereignty, as symbols which merely flatter their possessor
and misrepresent the implanted nature of man, whose

supposed splendour should be most fully displayed in him. The King's appeal to ceremony, 'Show me but thy worth!' voices a need for assurance which cannot be given. Its lack becomes a cause of neurotic anxiety and bitterness in plays that follow *Henry V*.

At the point where uncertainty over established values begins to obtrude upon Shakespeare's interest in man's political identity, the matter of the English chronicles can no longer provide the groundwork of his imaginative interest. His attention is shifting from a world of fixed standards, where a usurper's attempts to assume sovereignty can be measured against an ideal of kingship, to an area of blurred values where the hero loses faith in his ability to judge or to act correctly. This shift of imaginative interest in Shakespeare is marked by a growing tendency to make private experience and rumination the centre of dramatic attention, as uncertainty forces the hero to explore himself, and to disclose the cryptic workings of individual being. The more obvious kinds of physical action, a basic element of the history-play, give way to this more absorbed preoccupation with the basis of human character and the hero's attempt to understand his own motives. In this imaginative context the image of the king is irrelevant to Shakespeare's major purposes, It was only in the Histories that he could become a central figure; an embodiment of the power and magnificence which man attributes to himself in ignorance of his deeply divided nature.

INDEX

Index

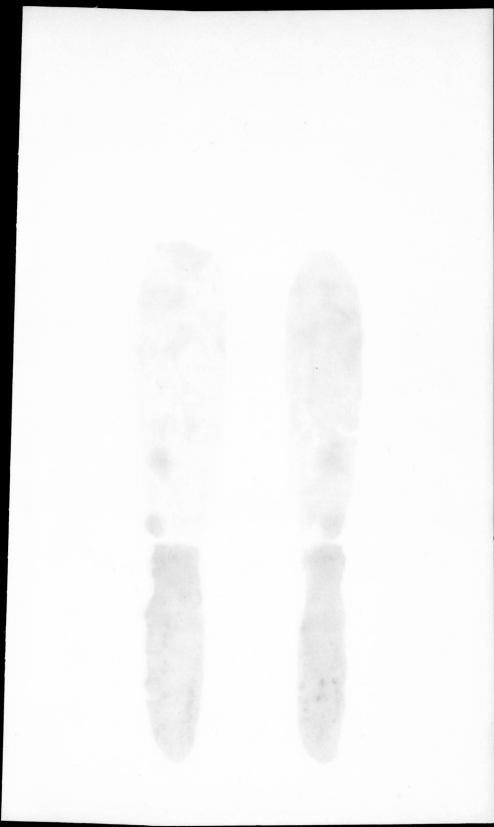

56587

PR
2982
W5

WINDY, JAMES
    THE PLAYER KING.